LOW-FAT
WAYS TO COOK
ONE-DISH
MEALS

LOW-FAT
WAYS TO COOK
ONE-DISH
MEALS

COMPILED AND EDITED BY
SUSAN M. McINTOSH, M.S., R.D.

Oxmoor
House®

Copyright 1995 by Oxmoor House, Inc.
Book Division of Southern Progress Corporation
P.O. Box 2463, Birmingham, Alabama 35201

Library of Congress Catalog Number: 95-67712
ISBN: 0-8487-2202-7
Manufactured in the United States of America
Second Printing 1996

Editor-in-Chief: Nancy J. Fitzpatrick
Editorial Director, Special Interest Publications: Ann H. Harvey
Senior Foods Editor: Katherine M. Eakin
Senior Editor, Editorial Services: Olivia Kindig Wells
Art Director: James Boone

Low-Fat Ways To Cook One-Dish Meals

Menu and Recipe Consultant: Susan McEwen McIntosh, M.S., R.D.
Assistant Editor: Kelly Hooper Troiano
Copy Editor: Catherine Hamrick
Editorial Assistant: Julie A. Cole
Foods Editor: Cathy A. Wesler, R.D.
Indexer: Mary Ann Laurens
Assistant Art Director: Cynthia R. Cooper
Designer: Carol Damsky
Senior Photographer: Jim Bathie
Photographers: Howard L. Puckett, *Cooking Light* magazine;
  Ralph Anderson
Senior Photo Stylist: Kay E. Clarke
Photo Stylists: Cindy Manning Barr, *Cooking Light* magazine;
  Virginia R. Cravens
Production and Distribution Director: Phillip Lee
Production Manager: Gail Morris
Associate Production and Distribution Manager: John Charles Gardner
Associate Production Manager: Theresa L. Beste
Production Assistant: Marianne Jordan

Our appreciation to the staff of *Cooking Light* magazine for their
contributions to this book.

Cover: *Garden Medley Pizza with Oatmeal Crust (Recipe follows on page 50)*
Frontispiece: *Curried Steak with Baby Vegetables (Recipe follows on page 78)*

CONTENTS

MAKE IT ONE DISH

*H*ealth-conscious Americans have realized that serving one-dish meals is not only more economical but also makes sense nutritionally. So, why not try replacing the traditional whole steak or chop plus two side dishes with smaller portions of meat combined with vegetables and pasta, rice, or bread? From skillet dishes to pizza, stir-fries to stews, the possibilities are endless.

WHAT'S A ONE-DISH MEAL?

For years, people across the world have depended on one-dish meals to stretch protein foods that were not always plentiful. The Mexicans combine meat, vegetables, and tortillas into fajitas, burritos, and tacos. Italians make their classic dish, lasagna, by layering meat, cheese, pasta, and tomato sauce. Stir-fries of meat, fish, or poultry with seasoned vegetables over rice are traditional one-dish meals of Oriental origin. Protein-rich black beans are simmered with other vegetables and served over rice for a meatless Cuban specialty.

The recipes in *Low-Fat Ways To Cook One-Dish Meals* include these and other healthy combinations of protein-rich foods, starchy foods, and vegetables or fruits. With the addition of bread or a salad, each recipe is a complete meal.

All recipes provide at least 10 grams of protein per serving. Carbohydrate comes from ½ cup rice, pasta, cereal, or other starchy food and ½ cup fruit or vegetable per serving. (Vegetables such as corn and potatoes may serve as the starch or the vegetable.)

To see how this works, look at the Garden Medley Pizza with Oatmeal Crust on page 50 (pictured on cover). Each serving is a meal in itself, providing protein from the reduced-fat cheese and carbohydrate from the oatmeal crust. You'll get plenty of nutrients from the broccoli, squash, and mushrooms.

ONE-DISH BENEFITS

- **Economical!**

Our parents and grandparents tried to stretch their dollars every time they planned meals and shopped for groceries. And we can follow their example. Make a pound of meat go further by using less expensive vegetables, pasta, rice, or bread—that's the concept behind many of our one-dish-meal casseroles, stews, stir-fries, salads, and sandwiches.

- **Timesaving!**

One-dish meals cut time. By cooking all the ingredients in one dish, you'll have fewer dishes to wash. And often, one-dish meals can be assembled ahead and refrigerated or even frozen. To facilitate last-minute preparation of main-dish salads and stir-fries, slice the vegetables ahead of time.

- **Nutritious!**

One of the most important benefits of one-dish meals is their nutritional value. Because less meat is used per serving than in typical meals, the fat content of the dish is decreased. Whole grain bread, cereal, rice, pasta, vegetables, and fruit all contribute complex carbohydrates, which provide vitamins, minerals, and fiber but very little fat.

The importance of dietary fiber, an essential part of a healthy diet, should not be ignored. It can help lower blood cholesterol levels and may help reduce the risk of colon cancer. (Simple carbohydrates, better known as sugars, do not provide fiber.)

Health advisory groups such as the American Heart Association and The American Dietetic Association recommend that at least 50 percent of our daily calories come from carbohydrates. Adults should consume at least six servings of breads, cereal, rice, or pasta and at least five servings of fruits and vegetables each day to reach this goal.

There is plenty of protein in one-dish meals. According to the AHA guidelines, about 20 percent of total daily calories should come from protein, which is abundant in meat, poultry, fish, and eggs and is also prevalent in skim milk, reduced-fat cheese and yogurt, dried beans, peas, legumes, and bean curd (tofu). Breads, cereal, rice, and pasta also contain protein.

Low-Fat Cooking Tips

As you try various recipes in this book, you will use cooking techniques basic to low-fat cooking.

• Buy only the leanest cuts of beef, pork, lamb, and veal. Select cuts such as beef tenderloin, beef round, beef sirloin, pork tenderloin, pork loin chop, cured or fresh ham, leg of lamb, lamb loin chops, and veal cutlets. Trim meat of all visible fat before cooking.

• Trim fat and remove the skin of chicken and turkey before or after cooking.

• Marinate lean meats, fish, and poultry in fat-free or low-fat marinades to enhance their flavors. Reduce or omit oil from marinade recipes by substituting water or broth. Other low-fat ingredients for marinades include citrus juices, wines, and flavored vinegars.

• Roast meats and poultry on a rack in a broiler pan so fat can drip away. For easier cleanup, coat broiler pan with vegetable cooking spray before cooking.

• Brown ground meat in a nonstick skillet or in a skillet coated with vegetable cooking spray. In addition to lean ground beef, try ground turkey or chicken. After cooking the meat, place it in a colander to drain excess fat. To further reduce the fat, pat the cooked meat dry with paper towels after draining, and wipe drippings from the skillet with a paper towel before continuing to cook.

• Cook pasta, rice, grains, and green and starchy vegetables with little or no added fat. Steaming, sautéing, and stir-frying are best for cooking vegetables because these require a minimum of fat while preserving nutrients. Use a nonstick skillet or wok or a skillet coated with vegetable cooking spray for sautéing and stir-frying.

• Coat baking dishes, pans, and casseroles with vegetable cooking spray instead of butter, oil, or shortening. To add more flavor to foods, use olive oil-flavored or butter-flavored cooking spray.

• Make soups, stews, stocks, or broths ahead of time and chill overnight in the refrigerator. After the soup has chilled, skim off the hardened fat with a spoon, discard the fat, and then reheat.

If there is no time to chill the soup, skim off as much fat as possible, and add several ice cubes to the warm liquid. The fat will cling to the ice cubes, which can then be removed and discarded.

A fat-off ladle and fat-separating cup are two handy tools to aid in removing unwanted fat from soup, broth, and meat drippings.

• Substitute skim milk when a recipe calls for cream or whole milk. And if the recipe doesn't look creamy enough, add nonfat dry milk 1 tablespoon at a time until desired consistency is reached.

• Use reduced-fat cheese and nonfat sour cream and yogurt. Since many of the reduced-fat cheeses are still over 50 percent fat, try to substitute a strong-flavored cheese and use less of it. You'll get the cheese flavor but without all the fat.

When cooking with yogurt, keep temperature low and heating time short to prevent separation.

• Decrease butter, margarine, vegetable oil, and shortening. Eliminate added fat in pasta, rice, and vegetables, and decrease the amount called for in the recipe. When fat is decreased, you may need to add a liquid such as water, fruit juice, or skim milk to make up for moisture loss.

Although margarine and vegetable oils contain about the same number of fat grams and calories as butter, they are lower in saturated fat and cholesterol and are therefore healthier choices.

Use reduced-fat margarine for some recipes but not baked goods unless specified; the water that is whipped into reduced-calorie margarine may cause sogginess.

• Substitute 2 egg whites or ¼ cup egg substitute for a whole egg to reduce cholesterol.

MEAL PLANNING

A healthy meal plan includes daily servings of a variety of each of the following food groups:
- Breads, cereal, rice, and pasta (6 to 11 servings)
- Vegetables (3 to 5 servings)
- Fruit (2 to 4 servings)
- Milk, yogurt, and cheese (2 to 3 servings)
- Meats, poultry, fish, dry beans, eggs, and nuts (2 to 3 servings)

It's easy to plan a complete menu around one-dish meal recipes—a starch, a vegetable or fruit, and a protein-rich ingredient are already in each dish. You may need only a salad or soup to round out your meal. But to get in a healthy six servings of bread, cereal, rice, or pasta a day, you will probably want to also add low-fat bread to most meals. Fruit and yogurt are good choices for dessert. Skim milk and water are excellent beverage choices.

The foods selected should have complementary tastes. Plan to serve only one highly seasoned or strong-flavored item in each meal. And don't repeat flavors. If your casserole contains tomatoes or tomato sauce, don't include tomatoes in the salad. Appearance is important, too. Foods come in many colors, so include a variety with each meal. And don't forget that garnishes, such as orange twists or even parsley sprigs, help to make a plate visually appealing. Look for other garnishing ideas in the photographs throughout this book.

The texture, shape, and size of the ingredients and finished dishes you plan to serve should also contrast. Some casseroles have a soft texture; complement them with a crisp vegetable or fruit salad. If the stir-fry you prepare contains strips of peppers and beef, choose a salad of simple greens. If your main-dish stew is composed of small chopped vegetables, make sure that the salad doesn't contain small pieces.

Strive to vary the temperature of foods in a meal as well. Cold soups, chilled fruit, and vegetable salads provide welcome contrasts to hot entrées.

Round Out One-Dish Meals

Here's a list of quick, low-fat bread and salad ideas to help you complete your one-dish meals.

BREADS
- French or Italian bread or rolls
- Whole wheat, onion, sesame seed, or poppy seed bagels
- Cornbread, corn sticks, or corn muffins
- Sourdough rolls or bread
- Whole wheat rolls
- English muffins
- Pita bread
- Warm flour tortillas
- Breadsticks
- Cracker bread
- Melba toast
- Oyster crackers

SALADS
- Bibb lettuce with a reduced-fat vinaigrette
- Packaged shredded cabbage with commercial reduced-fat coleslaw dressing
- Simple spinach or tossed salad with reduced-fat commercial salad dressing (packaged salads are available in the produce section of the supermarket)
- Sliced tomatoes over Bibb or other lettuce leaves
- Grated carrots with raisins and low-fat pineapple yogurt
- Sliced cucumbers marinated in reduced-fat Italian salad dressing
- Chilled baby carrots and celery sticks
- Steamed asparagus marinated in reduced-fat vinaigrette or Italian salad dressing
- Torn romaine lettuce with reduced-fat Caesar salad dressing
- Cauliflower flowerets tossed with reduced-fat creamy Italian salad dressing
- Sliced fresh mushrooms and zucchini marinated in reduced-fat herb salad dressing
- Mandarin orange sections or fresh strawberries tossed with torn lettuce and balsamic vinegar
- Assorted fresh fruit salad with reduced-fat poppy seed dressing
- Slices of fresh cantaloupe, honeydew, or other melon, sprinkled with chopped fresh mint
- Assorted fresh berries, topped with low-fat vanilla yogurt
- Simple Waldorf salad of chopped apples, raisins, chopped celery, and reduced-fat mayonnaise

LOW-FAT BASICS

*W*hether you are trying to lose or maintain weight, low-fat eating makes good sense. Research studies show that decreasing your fat intake reduces risks of heart disease, diabetes, and some types of cancer. The goal recommended by major health groups is an intake of 30 percent or less of total daily calories.

The *Low-Fat Ways To Cook* series gives you practical, delicious recipes with realistic advice about low-fat cooking and eating. The recipes are lower in total fat than traditional recipes, and most provide less than 30 percent of calories from fat and less than 10 percent of calories from saturated fat.

If you have one high-fat item during a meal, you can balance it with low-fat choices for the rest of the day and still remain within the recommended percentage. For example, fat contributes 45 percent of the calories in Broccoli-Cauliflower Tossed Salad for the Western Roundup supper menu on page 19. However, because the salad is combined with other low-fat foods, the total menu provides only 11 percent of calories as fat.

The goal of fat reduction need not be to eliminate all fat from your diet. In fact, a small amount of fat is needed to transport fat-soluble vitamins and maintain other normal body functions.

FIGURING THE FAT

The easiest way to achieve a diet with 30 percent or fewer of total calories from fat is to establish a daily "fat budget" based on the total number of calories you need each day. To estimate your daily calorie requirements, multiply your current weight by 15. Remember that this is only a rough guide because calorie requirements vary according to age, body size, and level of activity. To gain or lose 1 pound a week, add or subtract 500 calories a day. (A diet of fewer than 1,200 calories a day is not recommended unless medically supervised.)

Once you determine your personal daily caloric requirement, it's easy to figure the number of fat grams you should consume each day. These should equal or be lower than the number of fat grams indicated on the Daily Fat Limits chart.

DAILY FAT LIMITS		
Calories Per Day	30 Percent of Calories	Grams of Fat
1,200	360	40
1,500	450	50
1,800	540	60
2,000	600	67
2,200	660	73
2,500	750	83
2,800	840	93

NUTRITIONAL ANALYSIS

Each recipe in *Low-Fat Ways To Cook One-Dish Meals* has been kitchen-tested by a staff of qualified home economists. Registered dietitians have determined the nutrient information, using a computer system that analyzes every ingredient. These efforts ensure the success of each recipe and will help you fit these recipes into your own meal planning.

The nutrient grid that follows each recipe provides calories per serving and the percentage of calories from fat. In addition, the grid lists the grams of total fat, saturated fat, protein, and carbohydrate, and the milligrams of cholesterol and sodium per serving. The nutrient values are as accurate as possible and are based on these assumptions.

• When the recipe calls for cooked pasta, rice, or noodles, the analysis is based on cooking without additional salt or fat.

• The calculations indicate that meat and poultry are trimmed of fat and skin before cooking.

• Only the amount of marinade absorbed by the food is calculated.

• Garnishes and other optional ingredients are not calculated.

• Some of the alcohol calories evaporate during heating, and only those remaining are counted.

• When a range is given for an ingredient (3 to 3½ cups, for instance), the lesser amount is calculated.

• Fruits and vegetables listed in the ingredients are not peeled unless specified.

SENSIBLE DINNERS

*L*ate afternoon traffic does not back up, dinner magically appears on the table, and you read the newspaper before eight o'clock—feet propped on your favorite ottoman. In your dreams! However, this fantasy can come true, at least in part, with these menus that are designed to help you get a complete meal on the table with ease. These one-dish meals can remain just that, but we have provided some easy dinner accompaniments. For Mustard-Honey Glazed Ham Kabobs (page 17), we suggest a low-fat Caesar salad and an easy-to-make bread. And don't forget dessert—the double-chocolate pudding is a sure hit.

Clockwise: *Mediterranean Pizza Loaf, Pepperoncini-Cheese Dip, and Spicy Orange Salad (Menu follows on page 12)*

DINNER WITH INTERNATIONAL FLAIR
(pictured on page 10)

This menu creates a cosmopolitan atmosphere with all the comforts of home. Start with an Italian-flavored dip and breadsticks (2 tablespoons dip and 2 breadsticks per serving). Lamb, eggplant, oregano, and feta cheese lend a distinct Greek flavor to the pizza, and the salad features two Mexican staples—oranges and cilantro. Then come back to Italy for a dessert of lightened cappuccino.

Pepperoncini-Cheese Dip

Commercial breadsticks

Mediterranean Pizza Loaf

Spicy Orange Salad

Frosty Cappuccino

———

Serves 4
TOTAL CALORIES PER SERVING: 720
(CALORIES FROM FAT: 18.3%)

PEPPERONCINI-CHEESE DIP

¼ cup 1% low-fat cottage cheese
¼ cup plus 2 tablespoons light process cream cheese product
¼ cup nonfat sour cream alternative
¼ cup canned finely chopped pepperoncini peppers, drained
1 tablespoon grated Parmesan cheese
⅛ teaspoon garlic powder
Pepperoncini pepper (optional)

Combine first 3 ingredients in container of an electric blender; cover and process until smooth.

Transfer to a bowl; stir in chopped peppers, Parmesan cheese, and garlic powder. Garnish with a pepperoncini pepper, if desired. Serve with commercial breadsticks. Yield: 1 cup.

PER TABLESPOON: 19 CALORIES (47% FROM FAT)
FAT 1.0G (SATURATED FAT 0.6G)
PROTEIN 1.4G   CARBOHYDRATE 0.8G
CHOLESTEROL 3MG   SODIUM 85MG

MEDITERRANEAN PIZZA LOAF

6 ounces lean ground lamb
½ cup chopped onion
2 cloves garlic, minced
2½ cups peeled, cubed eggplant
1 cup sliced fresh mushrooms
¼ cup water
1 teaspoon dried oregano, divided
⅓ cup no-salt-added tomato paste
1 (1-pound) loaf French bread
½ cup frozen artichoke hearts, thawed and chopped
3 tablespoons crumbled feta cheese

Combine first 3 ingredients in a medium-size nonstick skillet; cook over medium heat until browned, stirring until meat crumbles. Drain and pat dry with paper towels. Wipe drippings from skillet with a paper towel.

Place skillet over medium-high heat until hot. Add eggplant and mushrooms; sauté 2 minutes. Stir in water and ¾ teaspoon oregano. Cover, reduce heat, and simmer 5 minutes or until vegetables are tender. Add lamb mixture and tomato paste, stirring well; cook 1 minute or until thoroughly heated.

Slice bread in half lengthwise. Place one half, cut side up, on a baking sheet. Reserve remaining half for another use. Broil 5½ inches from heat (with electric oven door partially opened) 1½ minutes or until lightly toasted. Spoon lamb mixture evenly over bread. Top with artichoke hearts, cheese, and remaining ¼ teaspoon oregano. Broil 5½ inches from heat (with electric door partially opened) 3 minutes or until cheese softens. Cut into 4 equal pieces, and serve immediately. Yield: 4 servings.

PER SERVING: 323 CALORIES (18% FROM FAT)
FAT 6.5G (SATURATED FAT 2.4G)
PROTEIN 18.7G   CARBOHYDRATE 47.6G
CHOLESTEROL 37MG   SODIUM 488MG

SPICY ORANGE SALAD

2 tablespoons unsweetened orange juice
2 tablespoons white vinegar
2 teaspoons olive oil
⅛ teaspoon ground coriander
⅛ teaspoon ground cumin
⅛ teaspoon ground red pepper
1 medium head Bibb lettuce, separated into leaves
1 cup watercress sprigs
1 tablespoon minced fresh cilantro
2 cups orange sections (about 6 oranges)
Fresh cilantro sprigs (optional)

Combine first 6 ingredients; stir with a wire whisk. Arrange lettuce and watercress on 4 salad plates; sprinkle with minced cilantro. Top evenly with orange sections. Drizzle vinegar mixture evenly over salads. Garnish with cilantro sprigs, if desired. Yield: 4 servings.

PER SERVING: 79 CALORIES (28% FROM FAT)
FAT 2.5G (SATURATED FAT 0.3G)
PROTEIN 1.5G   CARBOHYDRATE 14.4G
CHOLESTEROL 0MG   SODIUM 5MG

FROSTY CAPPUCCINO

¼ cup ground coffee
2 teaspoons unsweetened cocoa
2 teaspoons grated orange rind
¼ teaspoon ground cinnamon
1¾ cups water
1 cup 1% low-fat milk
¼ cup plus 2 tablespoons firmly packed brown sugar
2 tablespoons Kahlúa or other coffee-flavored liqueur

Combine first 4 ingredients in coffee filter or filter basket of a drip coffee maker. Add water to coffee maker. Prepare coffee according to manufacturer's instructions. Transfer to a pitcher. Stir in milk and remaining ingredients. Pour into ice cube trays; freeze until firm.

Position knife blade in food processor bowl. Add coffee ice cubes; process 2 minutes. Serve immediately. Yield: 4 (1-cup) servings.

PER SERVING: 134 CALORIES (5% FROM FAT)
FAT 0.8G (SATURATED FAT 0.5G)
PROTEIN 2.4G   CARBOHYDRATE 26.2G
CHOLESTEROL 2MG   SODIUM 41MG

Did You Know?

Don't be tricked into spending money on magic formulas that promise quick and easy weight loss. People who lose weight by these methods inevitably gain it back. Exercising and eating sensibly are the surest and safest ways to lose weight and keep it off.

CASUAL SUMMER SUPPER

"Summertime and the living is easy" . . . especially when you plan a relaxed supper with friends. Spicy Tuna-Pasta Toss is a refreshing one-dish salad that can be made ahead. Both the muffins and dessert take advantage of fresh seasonal produce. The dessert is one you'll want to try often during the summer—it's delicious, yet simple to make.

Spicy Tuna-Pasta Toss

Zucchini Muffins

Gingered Peach Sundaes

Iced tea

Serves 6
TOTAL CALORIES PER SERVING: 717
(CALORIES FROM FAT: 23%)

Spicy Tuna-Pasta Toss and Zucchini Muffins

SPICY TUNA-PASTA TOSS

9 ounces tri-colored corkscrew pasta,
    uncooked
3 (6⅛-ounce) cans chunk white tuna in spring
    water, drained
¾ cup sweet yellow pepper strips
¾ cup quartered cherry tomatoes
¼ cup plus 2 tablespoons diced celery
1 cup plus 2 tablespoons no-salt-added salsa
¾ cup reduced-calorie mayonnaise
¾ teaspoon ground red pepper
Curly leaf lettuce leaves (optional)
3 tablespoons sliced green onions

Cook pasta according to package directions, omitting salt and fat. Drain; rinse under cold water, and drain. Combine pasta, tuna, and next 3 ingredients.

Combine salsa, mayonnaise, and red pepper. Add to pasta mixture; toss. Cover and chill. Serve in a lettuce-lined bowl, if desired; sprinkle with green onions. Yield: 6 (1½-cup) servings.

PER SERVING: 359 CALORIES (27% FROM FAT)
FAT 10.8G (SATURATED FAT 0.5G)
PROTEIN 25.5G   CARBOHYDRATE 37.7G
CHOLESTEROL 40MG   SODIUM 620MG

ZUCCHINI MUFFINS

¾ cup all-purpose flour
¼ cup yellow cornmeal
¾ teaspoon baking powder
¼ teaspoon baking soda
⅛ teaspoon salt
⅛ teaspoon ground cumin
1 cup shredded zucchini
2 tablespoons vegetable oil
2½ tablespoons honey
1 egg white, lightly beaten
1 teaspoon skim milk
Vegetable cooking spray

Combine first 6 ingredients; stir. Add zucchini to flour mixture; make a well in center of mixture. Combine oil, honey, egg white, and milk; add to dry ingredients, stirring just until dry ingredients are moistened.

Spoon batter into muffin pans coated with cooking spray, filling two-thirds full. Bake at 375° for 20 minutes or until golden. Yield: 6 muffins.

Note: This recipe may be doubled easily. For freezing instructions refer to page 21.

PER MUFFIN: 153 CALORIES (30% FROM FAT)
FAT 5.1G (SATURATED FAT 0.9G)
PROTEIN 3.0G   CARBOHYDRATE 24.6G
CHOLESTEROL 0MG   SODIUM 112MG

GINGERED PEACH SUNDAES

3 medium-size fresh peaches, peeled and sliced
2 tablespoons chopped almonds
1 tablespoon brown sugar
1 tablespoon minced crystallized ginger
1 tablespoon lemon juice
1 tablespoon reduced-calorie margarine,
    melted
3 cups vanilla nonfat frozen yogurt

Combine first 6 ingredients in a large nonstick skillet. Cook over medium heat 8 to 10 minutes or until peaches are tender, stirring frequently. Scoop ½ cup frozen yogurt into each of 6 dessert dishes. Top each with ¼ cup peach mixture. Serve immediately. Yield: 6 servings.

PER SERVING: 146 CALORIES (15% FROM FAT)
FAT 2.5G (SATURATED FAT 0.3G)
PROTEIN 4.4G   CARBOHYDRATE 28.9G
CHOLESTEROL 0MG   SODIUM 81MG

Quick Tip

Add some spark to iced tea with fresh mint leaves, lemon slices, and a dash of sparkling mineral water—several flavored varieties are available.

Mustard-Honey Glazed Ham Kabobs

ELEGANT DINNER

Do you like to entertain but feel too busy to create a complicated menu? This dinner is a snap because you can put it together quickly. Get a head start by preparing the dessert early in the day. Begin the dinner preparation by toasting bagel slices for the salad. While they bake, assemble the kabobs. Cook the rice, season the bread, and broil the kabobs during the last 30 minutes.

Mustard-Honey Glazed Ham Kabobs

Tangy Caesar Salad

Herbed Bruschetta

Double-Chocolate Satin Pudding

Sparkling mineral water

Serves 4
TOTAL CALORIES PER SERVING: 792
(CALORIES FROM FAT 16%)

MUSTARD-HONEY GLAZED HAM KABOBS

¼ cup honey
¼ cup bourbon or unsweetened orange juice
3 tablespoons Dijon mustard
1 teaspoon peeled, minced gingerroot
1 clove garlic, minced
32 snow pea pods (about 6 ounces), trimmed
1 small fresh pineapple, peeled and cored
2 medium-size sweet red peppers, seeded and cut into 32 (1-inch) pieces
¾ pound lean, low-salt cooked ham, cut into 24 (1-inch) cubes
Vegetable cooking spray
2 cups cooked long-grain rice (cooked without salt or fat)

Combine first 5 ingredients in a small bowl; stir well, and set aside.

Arrange snow peas in a vegetable steamer over boiling water. Cover; steam 2 to 3 minutes or until crisp-tender. Place in ice water until cool; drain.

Cut fresh pineapple into 32 (1-inch) cubes, reserving remaining pineapple for another use. Wrap 1 snow pea around each pineapple cube. Thread 4 pineapple cubes, 4 red pepper pieces,

and 3 ham cubes alternately onto each of 8 (12-inch) skewers.

Place kabobs on rack of a broiler pan coated with cooking spray. Brush kabobs with mustard mixture. Broil 5½ inches from heat (with electric oven door partially opened) 3 minutes. Turn and baste with remaining mustard mixture; broil an additional 3 to 4 minutes or until kabobs are thoroughly heated.

Place rice on a large serving platter. Arrange kabobs over rice. Serve warm. Yield: 4 servings.

PER SERVING: 406 CALORIES (13% FROM FAT)
FAT 5.9G (SATURATED FAT 2.9G)
PROTEIN 19.5G   CARBOHYDRATE 62.4G
CHOLESTEROL 42MG   SODIUM 998MG

Grilling Directions: Follow directions for assembling kabobs. Coat grill rack with cooking spray; place on grill over medium-hot coals (350° to 400°). Brush kabobs with mustard mixture. Place kabobs on rack; grill, uncovered, 3 minutes. Turn kabobs, and baste with remaining mustard mixture. Grill an additional 3 to 4 minutes or until kabobs are thoroughly heated.

Tangy Caesar Salad

1 onion-flavored bagel
Butter-flavored vegetable cooking spray
4 cups torn romaine lettuce (about ½ large
   head)
1 tablespoon freshly grated Parmesan cheese
½ teaspoon coarsely ground pepper
1 tablespoon lemon juice
1 teaspoon low-sodium Worcestershire sauce
¾ teaspoon red wine vinegar
¼ teaspoon dry mustard
⅛ teaspoon garlic powder
3 tablespoons plain nonfat yogurt

   Cut bagel into 2 half-circles using a serrated
knife. Cut each half-circle horizontally into ¼-inch-
thick slices. Place bagel slices on a baking sheet;
coat with cooking spray. Bake at 300° for 25 minutes or until lightly browned and crisp; set aside.
   Combine lettuce, cheese, and pepper in a large
bowl; toss well. Combine lemon juice and next 4
ingredients, stirring well. Add yogurt; stir well. Add
to lettuce mixture; toss gently to coat.
   Break bagel chips into small pieces; add to lettuce mixture, and toss gently. Serve immediately.
Yield: 4 servings.

PER SERVING: 97 CALORIES (12% FROM FAT)
FAT 1.3G (SATURATED FAT 0.4G)
PROTEIN 4.6G   CARBOHYDRATE 16.6G
CHOLESTEROL 1MG   SODIUM 186MG

Menu Helper

   When entertaining, plan a meal that can be
prepared ahead of time. With this menu, you
could make the mustard glaze, cut up the ham
and vegetables for the kabobs, bake bagel
slices and wash lettuce for the salad, and cook
and chill the chocolate pudding—all before
your guests arrive. Then take it easy, and
enjoy the company.

Herbed Bruschetta

1 clove garlic, halved
4 (1-ounce) diagonally-cut slices French bread
   (about 1 inch thick), toasted
1 teaspoon extra-virgin olive oil
⅛ teaspoon dried rosemary, crushed
⅛ teaspoon dried thyme
⅛ teaspoon dried basil
Dash of coarsely ground pepper

   Rub garlic on one side of each bread slice; brush
with oil, and sprinkle with remaining ingredients.
Discard garlic. Serve warm or at room temperature.
Yield: 4 servings.

PER SERVING: 107 CALORIES (18% FROM FAT)
FAT 2.1G (SATURATED FAT 0.4G)
PROTEIN 3.1G   CARBOHYDRATE 18.6G
CHOLESTEROL 1MG   SODIUM 191MG

Double-Chocolate Satin Pudding

⅓ cup sugar
2 tablespoons cornstarch
2 tablespoons unsweetened cocoa
1 teaspoon instant espresso granules
⅛ teaspoon salt
1¾ cups 2% low-fat milk
1 (1-ounce) square semisweet chocolate,
   grated
1 teaspoon vanilla extract

   Combine first 5 ingredients in a saucepan; stir
well. Gradually add milk, stirring with a wire
whisk. Bring to a boil over medium heat, stirring
constantly. Add chocolate; cook 1 minute, stirring
constantly until chocolate melts. Remove from
heat; stir in vanilla. Pour pudding into individual
dessert dishes; cover and chill at least 2 hours.
Yield: 4 (½-cup) servings.

PER SERVING: 182 CALORIES (23% FROM FAT)
FAT 4.6G (SATURATED FAT 2.9G)
PROTEIN 4.8G   CARBOHYDRATE 31.2G
CHOLESTEROL 8MG   SODIUM 126MG

WESTERN ROUNDUP

Howdy, pilgrim. Looking for some rootin'-tootin' action on Saturday night? Get out your cowboy hat, and invite the crowd over for a western theme night. Rustle up a steaming bowl of Three Bean-Turkey Soup along with a tossed salad, and one wedge of bread per person. Serve the meal on TV trays as you watch *Stagecoach;* or, for a little excitement, tune in to *Gunfight at the O.K. Corral.* Before everybody hits the trail, offer warm rice pudding. Rowdy Yates never had it so good.

Three Bean-Turkey Soup

Broccoli-Cauliflower Tossed Salad

Whole Wheat and Rye Bread

Fruited Rice Pudding

Coffee

Serves 10

TOTAL CALORIES PER SERVING: 687

(CALORIES FROM FAT: 11%)

Three Bean-Turkey Soup, Broccoli-Cauliflower Tossed Salad, and Whole Wheat and Rye Bread

Three Bean-Turkey Soup

1 cup dried red kidney beans
1 cup dried Great Northern beans
1 cup dried black beans
8 cups water
Vegetable cooking spray
1 pound freshly ground raw turkey
1 cup chopped onion
¾ cup chopped green pepper
4 cloves garlic, minced
2 (14½-ounce) cans no-salt-added whole
    tomatoes, undrained and coarsely chopped
1 (8-ounce) can no-salt-added tomato sauce
1½ cups sliced carrot
2 teaspoons dried oregano
1 teaspoon dried thyme
½ teaspoon chicken-flavored bouillon granules
½ teaspoon salt
½ teaspoon pepper

Sort and wash beans; place in a large Dutch oven. Cover with water to a depth of 2 inches above beans; let soak overnight. Drain well.

Combine beans and 8 cups water in pan; bring to a boil. Cover, reduce heat, and simmer 1 hour. Drain beans, reserving 3 cups water. Transfer ⅓ cup beans to a small bowl; mash beans with a fork, making a paste.

Coat pan with cooking spray; place over medium-high heat until hot. Add turkey, onion, green pepper, and garlic; cook until turkey is browned and onion is tender, stirring until turkey crumbles. Drain turkey mixture, and pat dry with paper towels. Wipe drippings from pan with a paper towel.

Return turkey mixture to pan. Add drained beans, reserved 3 cups water, bean paste, tomato, and remaining ingredients; bring to a boil. Cover, reduce heat, and simmer 1 hour and 15 minutes or until beans are tender. Yield: 10 (1½-cup) servings.

Per Serving: 297 Calories (8% from Fat)
Fat 2.7g (Saturated Fat 0.8g)
Protein 25.2g   Carbohydrate 44.6g
Cholesterol 29mg   Sodium 217mg

Broccoli-Cauliflower Tossed Salad

Wash and cut the broccoli and cauliflower early in the day; then cover and refrigerate the vegetables until just before mealtime.

2½ cups fresh broccoli flowerets
2½ cups fresh cauliflower flowerets
5 cups torn Bibb lettuce
1 cup chopped sweet red pepper
¼ cup canned low-sodium chicken broth,
    undiluted
¼ cup water
1 clove garlic, minced
2 tablespoons lemon juice
1 tablespoon olive oil
1 to 1½ teaspoons crushed red pepper
¼ teaspoon salt
¼ teaspoon freshly ground black pepper

Arrange broccoli and cauliflower in a vegetable steamer over boiling water. Cover and steam 4 to 5 minutes or until vegetables are crisp-tender. Transfer vegetables to a large bowl. Add lettuce and sweet red pepper; toss gently.

Combine chicken broth and remaining ingredients in a small jar; cover tightly, and shake vigorously to blend. Pour chicken broth mixture over vegetable mixture; toss gently. Serve immediately. Yield: 10 (1-cup) servings.

Per Serving: 32 Calories (45% from Fat)
Fat 1.6g (Saturated Fat 0.2g)
Protein 1.5g   Carbohydrate 3.9g
Cholesterol 0mg   Sodium 68mg

WHOLE WHEAT AND RYE BREAD

2 packages dry yeast
1 cup warm water (105° to 115°)
1 cup nonfat buttermilk
½ cup molasses
¼ cup vegetable oil
2¼ cups whole wheat flour
¾ cup rye flour
3 tablespoons unsweetened cocoa
1 teaspoon caraway seeds
1 teaspoon salt
2¼ cups bread flour, divided
Vegetable cooking spray

Dissolve yeast in warm water in a large bowl; let stand 5 minutes. Add buttermilk, molasses, and vegetable oil; beat at medium speed of an electric mixer until well blended. Add whole wheat flour, rye flour, cocoa, caraway seeds, and salt; beat until well blended. Gradually stir in 2 cups plus 2 tablespoons bread flour to make a soft dough.

Sprinkle remaining 2 tablespoons bread flour evenly over work surface. Turn dough out onto floured surface, and knead until dough is smooth and elastic (about 5 minutes). Place dough in a large bowl coated with cooking spray, turning to coat top. Cover and let rise in a warm place (85°), free from drafts, 1 hour or until doubled in bulk.

Punch dough down; divide in half. Shape each portion into a round loaf. Let rest 10 minutes. Place each round on a baking sheet coated with cooking spray.

Cover and let rise in a warm place, free from drafts, 30 minutes or until doubled in bulk. Bake at 350° for 30 minutes or until loaves sound hollow when tapped. Remove loaves from baking sheets; cool on wire racks. Cut each loaf into 12 wedges. Yield: 24 servings.

PER SERVING: 143 CALORIES (18% FROM FAT)
FAT 2.9G (SATURATED FAT 0.6G)
PROTEIN 4.2G CARBOHYDRATE 25.7G
CHOLESTEROL 0MG SODIUM 112MG

FRUITED RICE PUDDING

4 cups plus 1 tablespoon skim milk, divided
¾ cup sugar
½ cup short-grain rice, uncooked
1 tablespoon cornstarch
2 eggs, lightly beaten
1½ cups canned pears in juice, drained and chopped
1½ teaspoons vanilla extract
Vegetable cooking spray
1 tablespoon brown sugar
½ teaspoon ground cinnamon

Combine 4 cups milk, sugar, and rice in a large saucepan; bring to a boil. Cover, reduce heat, and simmer 15 minutes, stirring occasionally.

Combine cornstarch and remaining 1 tablespoon milk in a small bowl. Gradually add to rice mixture, stirring constantly. Bring to a boil; cook 1 minute. Remove from heat. Gradually stir about one-fourth of rice mixture into eggs; add to remaining rice mixture, stirring constantly. Stir in pear and vanilla.

Pour mixture into a 2-quart baking dish coated with cooking spray. Combine brown sugar and cinnamon; sprinkle over rice mixture. Bake at 350° for 45 minutes. Yield: 10 servings.

PER SERVING: 168 CALORIES (8% FROM FAT)
FAT 1.4G (SATURATED FAT 0.5G)
PROTEIN 5.1G CARBOHYDRATE 33.1G
CHOLESTEROL 46MG SODIUM 66MG

FYI

Any leftover Whole Wheat and Rye Bread can be frozen successfully for 2 to 3 months. Let the bread cool completely; then wrap tightly in moisture-proof, vapor-proof paper or freezer bags. Keep your freezer set at 0° or lower for best results.

ALFRESCO SUPPER

Dine under the stars, listen to a little night music, and linger in good company. Early in the day, marinate the chicken and chill the mayonnaise mixture. One hour before dinner, prepare the chicken and vegetables. Serve with one roll per person.

**Grilled Chicken with
Roasted Vegetables**

Berries à l'Orange

Commercial French rolls

Iced tea

Serves 4
TOTAL CALORIES PER SERVING: 614
(CALORIES FROM FAT: 13%)

GRILLED CHICKEN WITH ROASTED VEGETABLES

2 tablespoons peeled, grated gingerroot
1 tablespoon minced garlic
½ cup balsamic vinegar
¼ cup plus 2 tablespoons low-sodium teriyaki
   sauce
2 tablespoons water
1½ tablespoons olive oil
¼ cup nonfat mayonnaise
4 (4-ounce) skinned, boned chicken breast
   halves
4 small round red potatoes, quartered
Vegetable cooking spray
2 ears yellow corn, each cut into 4 pieces
8 cloves garlic, peeled
2 small yellow squash, cut into 1-inch pieces
2 small onions, quartered
1 medium zucchini, cut into 1-inch pieces
1 medium-size sweet red pepper, seeded and
   cut into 1-inch pieces

Combine first 6 ingredients in a jar; cover, and shake vigorously. Add 1 tablespoon teriyaki mixture to mayonnaise; stir well. Cover and chill.

Pour ¼ cup teriyaki mixture into a heavy-duty, zip-top plastic bag. Set aside remaining teriyaki mixture. Add chicken to bag; seal bag, and shake until chicken is well coated. Marinate in refrigerator at least 8 hours, turning bag occasionally.

Place potato in a large bowl; add 1 tablespoon reserved teriyaki mixture, tossing well. Place potato in a large roasting pan coated with cooking spray. Bake at 400° for 5 minutes. Place corn in bowl; add 2 tablespoons reserved teriyaki mixture, tossing well. Add to potato, and bake 10 minutes.

Place garlic cloves and remaining ingredients in bowl; add remaining teriyaki mixture, and toss well. Add squash mixture to potato mixture, and bake an additional 35 minutes or until vegetables are tender, stirring frequently. Set aside.

Coat grill rack with cooking spray; place on grill over medium-hot coals (350° to 400°). Remove chicken from marinade. Place chicken on rack; grill, covered, 4 minutes on each side or until done. Arrange chicken and vegetables on serving plates. Serve with mayonnaise mixture. Yield: 4 servings.

PER SERVING: 358 CALORIES (19% FROM FAT)
FAT 7.5G (SATURATED FAT 1.5G)
PROTEIN 32.8G CARBOHYDRATE 41.6G
CHOLESTEROL 72MG SODIUM 592MG

BERRIES À L'ORANGE

2 tablespoons grated orange rind
¼ cup fresh orange juice
2 tablespoons Cointreau or other orange-
   flavored liqueur
2 teaspoons sugar
4 cups fresh strawberries, halved

Combine first 4 ingredients. Pour mixture over strawberries; toss gently. Cover and chill.

To serve, toss gently, and spoon evenly into individual dessert dishes. Yield: 4 servings.

PER SERVING: 92 CALORIES (6% FROM FAT)
FAT 0.6G (SATURATED FAT 0.0G)
PROTEIN 1.2G CARBOHYDRATE 19.2G
CHOLESTEROL 0MG SODIUM 2MG

Grilled Chicken with Roasted Vegetables

ALL-IN-ONE SALADS

*F*at can lurk in unexpected places: salads, for
instance. Surprised? Take a look at some typical main-dish
salads. Predictable ingredients such as olives, bacon, and
especially cheese can create salads that are 50, 60, or even
70 percent fat. In the next few pages, you'll find lightened
recipes for old-time favorites like chicken and tuna salads.
Nonfat versions of mayonnaise, sour cream, and yogurt
lower fat, while herbs, spices, and vinegars boost flavor.
Interesting combinations of low-fat meats, starches, and
vegetables make the salads nutritionally complete.

Country Garden Tortellini (Recipe follows on page 26)

COUNTRY GARDEN TORTELLINI

(pictured on page 24)

2 (9-ounce) packages fresh cheese-filled tortellini
1 cup sliced carrot
1 cup cherry tomatoes, halved
1 (8-ounce) package frozen asparagus spears, thawed and cut into 1-inch pieces
1 (6-ounce) package frozen snow pea pods, thawed
⅔ cup sliced radishes
1 small purple onion, thinly sliced and separated into rings
3 tablespoons water
2 tablespoons lemon juice
2 tablespoons cider vinegar
1½ tablespoons olive oil
1 teaspoon dried basil
½ teaspoon pepper
¼ teaspoon salt

Cook tortellini according to package directions, omitting salt and fat; drain. Rinse with cold water; drain well, and set aside. Arrange carrot in a vegetable steamer over boiling water. Cover and steam 3 to 5 minutes or until crisp-tender. Combine tortellini, carrot, and next 5 ingredients in a bowl.

Combine water and remaining ingredients; stir well. Pour over tortellini mixture, and toss gently. Cover and chill. Yield: 8 servings.

PER SERVING: 246 CALORIES (21% FROM FAT)
FAT 5.8G (SATURATED FAT 1.9G)
PROTEIN 12.5G   CARBOHYDRATE 48.8G
CHOLESTEROL 25MG   SODIUM 372MG

FYI

After you cook pasta for a salad, drain and briefly rinse it under cold water to cool the pasta and to keep the strands from sticking together after chilling.

ROAST BEEF AND FETTUCCINE SALAD

Reduced-calorie mayonnaise and oil-free dressing are the secrets to this low-fat salad. Since the horseradish mixture contains sodium, we advise not adding salt to the fettuccine during cooking.

6 ounces fettuccine, uncooked
2½ cups broccoli flowerets
1 cup diagonally sliced carrot
¾ cup diagonally sliced celery
⅓ cup commercial oil-free Italian dressing
⅓ cup reduced-calorie mayonnaise
2½ tablespoons prepared horseradish
½ teaspoon freshly ground pepper
12 cherry tomatoes, halved
½ pound cooked lean roast beef or other lean cut of beef

Break fettuccine in half; cook fettuccine according to package directions, omitting salt and fat. Drain and rinse under cold water; drain again. Set fettuccine aside.

Cook broccoli and carrot in a small amount of boiling water 6 minutes or until crisp-tender. Drain, plunge into ice water, and drain again.

Combine cooked fettuccine, broccoli, carrot, and celery in a large bowl. Combine Italian dressing, mayonnaise, horseradish, and pepper; stir well. Add to fettuccine mixture; toss gently. Gently stir in tomatoes.

Cut roast beef into ½-inch-thick slices and cut each slice into ½-inch strips. Add roast beef strips to salad before serving. Yield: 6 servings.

Note: If desired, use ½ pound fresh crabmeat, sliced cooked pork tenderloin, or grilled, sliced and skinned chicken breast instead of roast beef in the salad. Yield: 6 servings.

PER SERVING: 227 CALORIES (29% FROM FAT)
FAT 7.4G (SATURATED FAT 0.1G)
PROTEIN 13.2G   CARBOHYDRATE 29.7G
CHOLESTEROL 4MG   SODIUM 505MG

Roast Beef and Fettuccine Salad

WARM BEEF SALAD WITH HORSERADISH SAUCE

½ cup plain nonfat yogurt
¼ cup low-fat sour cream
2 teaspoons prepared horseradish
12 small unpeeled round red potatoes (about 1¾ pounds)
¼ teaspoon salt, divided
1 (1-pound) lean flank steak
Vegetable cooking spray
1½ cups thinly sliced unpeeled cucumber
¼ cup thinly sliced purple onion
12 red leaf lettuce leaves

Combine first 3 ingredients in a small bowl; stir well. Cover and chill.

Cook potatoes in boiling water 20 minutes or until tender; drain and cool. Cut potatoes in half, and place in a bowl. Sprinkle with ⅛ teaspoon salt; set aside.

Trim fat from steak. Sprinkle steak with remaining ⅛ teaspoon salt. Place steak on a rack coated with cooking spray, and place rack in a shallow roasting pan. Broil steak 3 inches from heat (with electric oven door partially opened) 6 minutes on each side or to desired degree of doneness. Cut steak diagonally across grain into thin slices.

Divide potato, steak, cucumber, and onion evenly among 6 lettuce-lined serving plates. Serve with horseradish dressing. Yield: 6 servings.

PER SERVING: 335 CALORIES (30% FROM FAT)
FAT 11.1G (SATURATED FAT 4.7G)
PROTEIN 23.4G   CARBOHYDRATE 38.3G
CHOLESTEROL 45MG   SODIUM 202MG

BEEF, BARLEY, AND SWEET RED PEPPER SALAD

1 (½-pound) boneless top round steak
Vegetable cooking spray
3 cups cooked pearl barley (cooked without salt or fat)
¾ cup julienne-sliced sweet red pepper
½ cup thinly sliced green onions
1 tablespoon prepared mustard
1 tablespoon olive oil
1 tablespoon low-sodium soy sauce
1 tablespoon white wine vinegar
½ teaspoon dried thyme
⅛ teaspoon white pepper
⅛ teaspoon salt
8 curly leaf lettuce leaves

Place steak on rack of a broiler pan coated with cooking spray. Broil 5 inches from heat (with electric oven door partially opened) 3 minutes on each side or to desired degree of doneness. Cut steak diagonally across grain into thin slices; cut slices into 2-inch pieces.

Combine steak, pearl barley, and next 9 ingredients in a bowl; toss well. Cover and chill. Serve on individual lettuce-lined salad plates. Yield: 4 (1¼-cup) servings.

PER SERVING: 264 CALORIES (24% FROM FAT)
FAT 7.0G (SATURATED FAT 1.5G)
PROTEIN 18.2G   CARBOHYDRATE 32.6G
CHOLESTEROL 36MG   SODIUM 277MG

Menu Helper

Serve main-dish salads often, especially in warm weather. Try the recipes in this chapter; then have fun creating your own.

As a general guide, add julienne-sliced beef, turkey, or ham (2 ounces per serving) to a green salad. Or mix the same amount of chicken or pork into your favorite low-fat potato salad. Create a main-dish pasta salad by adding cheese or cooked meat to a basic recipe. To enhance the flavor of cold leftover meat, heat it briefly in a nonstick skillet before adding it to the salad, even if the salad is chilled.

SPINACH SALAD WITH HAM AND GARLIC DRESSING

Enjoy this salad for lunch with crusty French bread, iced tea, and a bowl of fresh fruit for dessert.

¼ cup plus 2 tablespoons plain low-fat yogurt
¼ cup low-fat sour cream
2 tablespoons skim milk
1 teaspoon finely chopped fresh basil
1 teaspoon finely chopped fresh chives
½ teaspoon dried Italian seasoning
1 small clove garlic, minced
6 (1-ounce) slices white bread
1 large clove garlic, halved
Vegetable cooking spray
¼ cup sliced shallots
1 small clove garlic, minced
7 ounces thinly sliced reduced-fat low-salt deli ham, cut into ½-inch strips
8 cups tightly packed torn spinach
2 cups sliced fresh mushrooms
¾ pound unpeeled medium tomatoes, cut into ¼-inch-thick wedges

Combine first 7 ingredients in a bowl; stir well. Cover and chill 1 hour.

Arrange bread slices in a single layer on a baking sheet. Bake at 350° for 20 minutes or until lightly browned. Lightly rub cut side of garlic halves on both sides of each bread slice; discard garlic halves. Trim bread crusts and discard. Cut each bread slice into 4 triangles; set aside.

Coat a large nonstick skillet with cooking spray; place over medium heat until hot. Add shallots and 1 clove minced garlic; sauté 3 minutes. Add ham; sauté 3 minutes or until thoroughly heated. Remove from heat.

Combine spinach, mushrooms, and tomato in a large bowl. Add ham mixture, tossing gently. Serve salad with dressing and croutons. Yield: 6 servings.

PER SERVING: 184 CALORIES (23% FROM FAT)
FAT 4.6G (SATURATED FAT 1.7G)
PROTEIN 13.0G   CARBOHYDRATE 24.7G
CHOLESTEROL 22MG   SODIUM 482MG

TABBOULEH SALAD WITH PORK

Tabbouleh, a favorite Middle Eastern bulgur salad, traditionally contains chopped fresh mint, olive oil, and lemon juice.

1 (½-pound) pork tenderloin
Vegetable cooking spray
¾ cup bulgur (cracked wheat), uncooked
¾ cup boiling water
1 cup unpeeled, chopped tomato
1 cup peeled, chopped cucumber
¼ cup minced fresh mint
¼ cup minced fresh parsley
¼ cup thinly sliced green onions
1 tablespoon peeled, grated gingerroot
1 clove garlic, minced
3 tablespoons lemon juice
1 tablespoon olive oil
¼ teaspoon salt
Fresh parsley sprigs (optional)

Trim fat from pork tenderloin. Cut tenderloin crosswise into ¼-inch-thick slices; cut slices into bite-size pieces. Place on rack of a broiler pan coated with cooking spray. Broil 3 inches from heat (with electric oven door partially opened) 6 minutes or until done, turning after 3 minutes; let cool.

Combine bulgur and water in a large bowl; let stand 15 minutes or until liquid is absorbed.

Add tenderloin, tomato, and next 6 ingredients; stir well. Combine lemon juice, oil, and salt, stirring with a wire whisk. Add to bulgur mixture; stir well. Cover and chill. Garnish with parsley, if desired. Yield: 4 (1-cup) servings.

PER SERVING: 256 CALORIES (21% FROM FAT)
FAT 6.1G (SATURATED FAT 1.3G)
PROTEIN 17.7G   CARBOHYDRATE 32.3G
CHOLESTEROL 40MG   SODIUM 190MG

Curried Couscous-Chicken Salad

CURRIED COUSCOUS-CHICKEN SALAD

¾ cup water
½ teaspoon salt
½ teaspoon curry powder
⅔ cup couscous, uncooked
1 cup cubed cooked chicken breast (about ½ pound skinned, boned chicken)
½ cup drained canned garbanzo beans
½ cup chopped red cabbage
¼ cup sliced green onions
¼ cup thinly sliced celery
1 teaspoon grated orange rind
¼ teaspoon pepper
¼ cup plus 2 tablespoons unsweetened orange juice
2 teaspoons olive oil
Leaf lettuce leaves
Orange wedges, cut in half (optional)

Bring water, salt, and curry powder to a boil in a medium saucepan; stir in couscous. Remove from heat; let stand, covered, 5 minutes. Fluff with a fork. Add chicken and next 4 ingredients.

Combine orange rind and next 3 ingredients in a bowl; stir with a wire whisk until blended. Add to couscous mixture; toss well. Serve over lettuce leaves. Garnish with orange wedges, if desired. Yield: 3 (1-cup) servings.

Note: Salad may be covered and chilled until serving time, if desired.

PER SERVING: 300 CALORIES (17% FROM FAT)
FAT 5.8G (SATURATED FAT 1.1G)
PROTEIN 24.6G   CARBOHYDRATE 36.5G
CHOLESTEROL 48MG   SODIUM 501MG

CHICKEN-TORTELLINI SALAD WITH MINT PESTO

2 (4-ounce) skinned, boned chicken breast
    halves, cut into ½-inch pieces
1 tablespoon all-purpose flour
Vegetable cooking spray
½ cup minced shallots
½ cup thinly sliced green onions
2 cloves garlic, minced
1 cup Chablis or other dry white wine
¼ cup lemon juice
9 ounces fresh cheese tortellini (cooked
    without salt or fat)
½ cup sweet yellow pepper strips
½ cup sweet red pepper strips
⅛ teaspoon salt
Mint Pesto
Lettuce leaves

Toss chicken with flour. Coat a small skillet with
cooking spray; place over medium-high heat until
hot. Add chicken, and cook 3 minutes or until
browned. Remove chicken from skillet, and set
aside. Add shallots, green onions, and garlic to skillet, and sauté 2 minutes or until tender. Add wine
and lemon juice, and bring to a boil. Return chick-
en to skillet; reduce heat, and simmer, uncovered,
10 minutes or until liquid evaporates.

Combine cooked tortellini, chicken mixture,
pepper strips, salt, and Mint Pesto in a large bowl,
and toss well. Cover and chill 1 hour. Serve on a
lettuce-lined platter. Yield: 6 (1-cup) servings.

MINT PESTO
2 cloves garlic
1 cup packed fresh lemon mint or spearmint
    leaves
½ cup loosely packed fresh parsley sprigs
¼ cup canned no-salt-added chicken broth,
    undiluted
3 tablespoons grated Parmesan cheese
2 tablespoons coarsely chopped walnuts
1 tablespoon lemon juice
1 tablespoon olive oil
⅛ teaspoon ground white pepper

Position knife blade in food processor bowl. Drop
garlic through food chute with processor running;
process 10 seconds. Add mint; pulse until blended.
Add remaining ingredients; pulse until combined.
Yield: ¾ cup.

PER SERVING: 265 CALORIES (30% FROM FAT)
FAT 8.8G (SATURATED FAT 2.7G)
PROTEIN 18.2G   CARBOHYDRATE 28.8G
CHOLESTEROL 43MG   SODIUM 251MG

PASTA PRIMAVERA CHICKEN SALAD

¼ cup julienne-sliced carrot
¼ cup cubed sweet red pepper
¼ cup cubed green pepper
¼ cup fresh broccoli flowerets
1 cup radiatore (short, fat, rippled pasta),
    cooked without salt or fat
⅔ cup cubed cooked chicken breast
Vegetable cooking spray
2 tablespoons minced fresh onion
1 clove garlic, minced
⅓ cup white vinegar
1 teaspoon sugar
1 teaspoon dried oregano
½ teaspoon coarsely ground pepper
¼ teaspoon salt
1½ teaspoons olive oil
2 tablespoons freshly grated Parmesan cheese

Arrange carrot, peppers, and broccoli in a vegetable steamer over boiling water. Cover and steam
5 minutes or until crisp-tender. Combine pasta,
vegetable mixture, and chicken in a bowl; set aside.

Coat a small saucepan with cooking spray; place
over medium heat until hot. Add onion and garlic;
sauté until tender. Remove from heat; stir in vinegar and next 5 ingredients. Pour over pasta mixture;
toss well. Cover and chill. Sprinkle with cheese
before serving. Yield: 2 (1½-cup) servings.

PER SERVING: 353 CALORIES (22% FROM FAT)
FAT 8.6G (SATURATED FAT 2.4G)
PROTEIN 26.7G   CARBOHYDRATE 42.3G
CHOLESTEROL 53MG   SODIUM 462MG

CHICKEN-BASIL PASTA

½ cup nonfat mayonnaise
¼ cup nonfat sour cream alternative
2 tablespoons chopped fresh basil
2 tablespoons skim milk
1 tablespoon lemon juice
½ teaspoon salt
¼ teaspoon garlic powder
¼ teaspoon dry mustard
1 cup fresh broccoli flowerets
½ cup frozen English peas, thawed
4 cups cooked fettuccine (cooked without salt
   or fat)
3 cups cubed cooked chicken breast
4 ounces reduced-fat Cheddar cheese, cut into
   thin strips
1 cup chopped tomato
½ medium-size sweet red pepper, cut into very
   thin strips
¼ cup sliced green onions
Leaf lettuce leaves

Combine first 8 ingredients in a small bowl; stir well, and set aside.

Arrange broccoli and peas in a vegetable steamer over boiling water. Cover and steam 3 minutes or until crisp-tender; drain and cool.

Combine mayonnaise mixture, broccoli and peas, and next 6 ingredients in a large bowl; toss gently. Cover and chill thoroughly. Serve over lettuce leaves. Yield: 8 (1¼-cup) servings.

PER SERVING: 282 CALORIES (18% FROM FAT)
FAT 5.5G (SATURATED FAT 2.3G)
PROTEIN 28.1G   CARBOHYDRATE 28.2G
CHOLESTEROL 60MG   SODIUM 510MG

FYI

Flavored vinegars are welcome additions to many salads. For a tasteful gift, pour Blueberry Vinegar into a decorative jar and attach the recipe for Chicken-Pasta Salad with Blueberries to show how the vinegar can be used.

CHICKEN-PASTA SALAD WITH BLUEBERRIES

1 (9-ounce) package frozen French-cut green
   beans, thawed
3 cups shredded cooked chicken breast (about
   1½ pounds skinned, boned chicken)
3 cups cooked fusilli (spiral-shaped pasta),
   cooked without salt or fat
1 cup fresh blueberries
¾ cup thinly sliced celery
¼ cup thinly sliced green onions
2 tablespoons finely chopped fresh oregano
½ cup plus 2 tablespoons plain low-fat yogurt
¼ cup plus 1 tablespoon reduced-calorie
   mayonnaise
3 tablespoons Blueberry Vinegar
½ teaspoon salt
½ teaspoon coarsely ground pepper
Lettuce leaves (optional)

Place green beans between paper towels, and squeeze until barely moist. Combine green beans and next 6 ingredients in a large bowl; set aside.

Combine yogurt and next 4 ingredients in a bowl; stir well. Pour over chicken mixture; toss gently. Cover and chill 2 hours. Serve on a lettuce-lined plate, if desired. Yield: 6 (1½-cup) servings.

BLUEBERRY VINEGAR
1 cup fresh blueberries
2 cups white vinegar
2 tablespoons sugar

Place blueberries in a sterilized 1-quart glass jar. Combine vinegar and sugar in a nonaluminum saucepan over high heat. Cover and bring to a boil. Remove from heat, and pour vinegar mixture over blueberries. Cover and let stand at room temperature 3 days.

Strain blueberry mixture through layers of damp cheesecloth into jars; discard blueberries. Seal jars with a cork or other airtight lid. Yield: 2 cups.

PER SERVING: 321 CALORIES (21% FROM FAT)
FAT 7.5G (SATURATED FAT 1.7G)
PROTEIN 32.1G   CARBOHYDRATE 30.6G
CHOLESTEROL 78MG   SODIUM 385MG

Chicken-Pasta Salad with Blueberries

GRILLED FIESTA SALAD

3 (4-ounce) skinned, boned chicken breast
    halves
¼ cup plus 1 tablespoon lime juice, divided
Vegetable cooking spray
1 teaspoon olive oil
3 tablespoons chopped green onions
1 cup seeded, chopped yellow tomato
1 cup chopped sweet red pepper
2 tablespoons seeded, chopped jalapeño pepper
2 tablespoons water
2 teaspoons honey
2 cups loosely packed shredded red leaf lettuce
1 cup loosely packed shredded iceberg lettuce
1 cup loosely packed shredded Boston lettuce
1 (14½-ounce) can black beans, drained
¼ cup nonfat sour cream alternative

Place chicken in a heavy-duty, zip-top plastic bag; add 2 tablespoons lime juice. Seal bag, and shake until chicken is coated. Marinate in refrigerator 2 hours, turning bag occasionally.

Coat a large nonstick skillet with cooking spray; add olive oil. Place over medium-high heat until hot. Add green onions, and sauté 1 minute. Add tomato and chopped peppers; sauté 2 minutes. Add remaining 3 tablespoons lime juice, water, and honey; cook over medium heat until thoroughly heated. Remove tomato mixture from heat. Set aside, and keep warm.

Remove chicken from marinade; discard marinade. Coat grill rack with cooking spray; place on grill over medium-hot coals (350° to 400°). Place chicken on rack; grill, covered, 5 to 6 minutes on each side or until chicken is done. Cut chicken into thin slices. Set aside, and keep warm.

Combine lettuces in a bowl; toss well. Place 1 cup lettuce mixture on each individual salad plate. Top with black beans. Arrange chicken evenly over beans. Spoon tomato mixture over chicken; top each serving with 1 tablespoon sour cream. Yield: 4 servings.

PER SERVING: 249 CALORIES (17% FROM FAT)
FAT 4.6G (SATURATED FAT 0.9G)
PROTEIN 27.5G   CARBOHYDRATE 25.2G
CHOLESTEROL 54MG   SODIUM 223MG

SOUTHWESTERN TURKEY AND BLACK BEAN SALAD

If seasoned black beans are not available, use regular canned black beans, adding additional cilantro and pepper, if desired.

¾ teaspoon ground cumin
¾ teaspoon chili powder
⅛ teaspoon salt
⅛ teaspoon ground red pepper
1 pound turkey breast cutlets, cut into
    ½-inch-wide strips
Vegetable cooking spray
1½ cups tightly packed torn curly endive
1½ cups tightly packed torn romaine lettuce
1 cup fresh orange sections (about 2 oranges)
¼ cup chopped purple onion
1 (15-ounce) can seasoned black beans, rinsed
    and drained
⅓ cup chopped fresh cilantro
¼ cup fresh lime juice
2 tablespoons fresh orange juice
2 teaspoons vegetable oil
⅛ teaspoon salt
1 small clove garlic, minced
Dash of ground red pepper

Combine first 4 ingredients in a large zip-top plastic bag. Add turkey; seal bag, and shake to coat turkey with seasoning mixture. Coat a large nonstick skillet with cooking spray; place over medium-high heat until hot. Add turkey, and sauté 4 minutes or until lightly browned. Spoon into a large bowl; add endive and next 4 ingredients. Set aside.

Combine cilantro and remaining ingredients in a bowl; stir with a wire whisk. Add to turkey mixture, tossing gently to coat. Serve at room temperature. Yield: 4 (2¼-cup) servings.

PER SERVING: 278 CALORIES (16% FROM FAT)
FAT 5.0G (SATURATED FAT 1.1G)
PROTEIN 33.6G   CARBOHYDRATE 25.1G
CHOLESTEROL 68MG   SODIUM 443MG

Southwestern Turkey and Black Bean Salad

SMOKED TURKEY SALAD WITH BROWN AND WILD RICE

½ cup wild rice, uncooked
2½ cups water
½ cup brown rice, uncooked
12 ounces smoked turkey breast, cut into ¾-inch cubes
12 cherry tomatoes, quartered
½ medium-size green pepper, cut into very thin strips
¼ cup chopped green onions
2 tablespoons minced fresh parsley
3 tablespoons balsamic vinegar
1 tablespoon vegetable oil
1 teaspoon minced fresh ginger
1 clove garlic, crushed
Lettuce leaves
2 tablespoons sliced almonds, toasted

Rinse and drain wild rice. Place water in a medium saucepan; bring to a boil. Stir in wild rice and brown rice; cover, reduce heat, and simmer 50 minutes or until rice is tender.

Combine cooked rice, turkey, and next 4 ingredients in a large bowl. Combine vinegar, oil, ginger, and garlic in a small jar; cover tightly, and shake vigorously. Pour over turkey mixture. Toss well. Spoon mixture onto a large serving platter lined with lettuce leaves. Sprinkle with toasted almonds. Yield: 6 servings.

PER SERVING: 242 CALORIES (30% FROM FAT)
FAT 7.9G (SATURATED FAT 1.7G)
PROTEIN 18.2G   CARBOHYDRATE 25.8G
CHOLESTEROL 32MG   SODIUM 400MG

TURKEY-ORZO SALAD

4 cups cooked orzo (cooked without salt or fat)
1½ cups cubed reduced-fat, low-salt deli turkey breast (about ½ pound)
1½ cups chopped celery
1 cup dark seedless raisins
½ cup reduced-calorie spoonable salad dressing
½ cup plain nonfat yogurt
1 tablespoon tarragon white wine vinegar
1 teaspoon curry powder
½ teaspoon ground ginger
⅛ teaspoon salt
Lettuce leaves

Combine first 4 ingredients in a large bowl; toss well, and set aside.

Combine salad dressing and next 5 ingredients in a bowl, and stir well. Pour over turkey-orzo mixture, and toss well. Cover and chill. Serve over lettuce leaves. Yield: 8 (1-cup) servings.

PER SERVING: 298 CALORIES (16% FROM FAT)
FAT 5.4G (SATURATED FAT 0.9G)
PROTEIN 12.5G   CARBOHYDRATE 49.4G
CHOLESTEROL 5MG   SODIUM 388MG

Fat Alert

Beware of the extras that can make or break a low-fat salad.

Limit or avoid:	Feel free to use:
Regular salad dressing	Oil-free dressing
Regular cheese	Reduced-fat cheese
Olives	Mushrooms
Bacon bits	Low-fat ham
Chopped egg yolk	Chopped egg white
Sunflower seeds	Chopped vegetables
Avocado	Garbanzo beans
Croutons	Low-fat bagel chips

SALMON-ARTICHOKE SPINACH SALAD

¾ cup Chablis or other dry white wine,
    divided
½ cup plus 3 tablespoons water, divided
1 (¾-pound) salmon fillet
1½ teaspoons dried dillweed, divided
8 small unpeeled round red potatoes, quartered
8 cups loosely packed fresh spinach
1 (14-ounce) can quartered artichoke hearts,
    drained
3 tablespoons red wine vinegar
1 tablespoon Dijon mustard

Combine ½ cup wine and ½ cup water in a large skillet; bring to a boil. Add salmon, skin side down, and sprinkle with 1 teaspoon dillweed. Cover, reduce heat, and simmer 13 minutes or until salmon flakes easily when tested with a fork. Remove salmon from skillet, and discard cooking liquid. Using a fork, separate salmon into bite-size pieces, and set aside.

Arrange potato in a vegetable steamer over boiling water. Cover; steam 13 minutes or until tender.

Remove stems from spinach; tear spinach into bite-size pieces, and place in a bowl. Add potato and artichokes; toss gently. Add salmon; set aside.

Combine remaining ¼ cup wine, remaining 3 tablespoons water, remaining ½ teaspoon dillweed, vinegar, and mustard in a jar. Cover tightly, and shake vigorously. Pour over salad; toss gently. Serve immediately. Yield: 4 servings.

PER SERVING: 286 CALORIES (26% FROM FAT)
FAT 8.2G (SATURATED FAT 1.4G)
PROTEIN 25.6G   CARBOHYDRATE 30.1G
CHOLESTEROL 58MG   SODIUM 319MG

Salmon-Artichoke Spinach Salad

SALMON AND BEAN SLAW

1 cup plus 1 tablespoon Chablis or other dry
    white wine, divided
5 whole peppercorns
1 bay leaf
1 (½-pound) salmon fillet, skinned
2 cups coarsely shredded cabbage
½ cup chopped purple onion
¼ cup minced fresh dillweed
1 (15-ounce) can dark red kidney beans,
    drained and rinsed
2 tablespoons lemon juice
2 teaspoons prepared mustard
1 teaspoon olive oil
⅛ teaspoon white pepper

Combine 1 cup wine, peppercorns, and bay leaf
in a large skillet; bring to a boil. Add salmon;
cover, reduce heat, and simmer 10 minutes or until
fish flakes easily when tested with a fork. Drain
and flake salmon.

Combine salmon, cabbage, and next 3 ingredients in a bowl; toss. Combine remaining 1 tablespoon wine, lemon juice, and remaining ingredients; stir well. Add to salmon mixture; toss gently.
Cover and chill. Yield: 3 (2-cup) servings.

PER SERVING: 235 CALORIES (32% FROM FAT)
FAT 8.3G (SATURATED FAT 1.4G)
PROTEIN 21.0G   CARBOHYDRATE 18.9G
CHOLESTEROL 49MG   SODIUM 372MG

TUNA-ORZO SALAD

¾ cup plus 3 tablespoons orzo, uncooked
2 cups unpeeled chopped plum tomato
½ cup (2 ounces) crumbled feta cheese
¼ cup chopped purple onion
2 tablespoons sliced ripe olives
1 (6½-ounce) can chunk light tuna in water,
    drained
½ cup red wine vinegar
2 tablespoons water
1½ tablespoons olive oil
½ teaspoon dried basil
½ teaspoon dried oregano
1 clove garlic, minced

Cook orzo according to package directions, omitting salt and fat. Combine orzo and next 5 ingredients in a large bowl; toss well.

Combine vinegar and remaining ingredients in
container of an electric blender; cover and process
until blended. Pour dressing over pasta mixture,
and toss well. Cover and chill, if desired. Yield: 4
(1½-cup) servings.

PER SERVING: 347 CALORIES (29% FROM FAT)
FAT 11.0G (SATURATED FAT 3.4G)
PROTEIN 21.0G   CARBOHYDRATE 40.9G
CHOLESTEROL 32MG   SODIUM 412MG

SEA SHELL SALAD

*To add a new twist to this salad, try serving it in
whole wheat pita bread halves with shredded lettuce.
One pita bread half has about 61 calories.*

8 ounces small shell macaroni, uncooked
1 cup shredded carrot
¾ cup diced green pepper
⅔ cup sliced celery
½ cup minced green onions
1 (6⅛-ounce) can tuna in water, drained and
    flaked
¼ cup plus 2 tablespoons plain low-fat yogurt
¼ cup reduced-calorie mayonnaise
¼ teaspoon celery seeds
¼ teaspoon salt
¼ teaspoon pepper
Curly leaf lettuce leaves

Cook macaroni according to package directions,
omitting salt and fat; drain. Rinse with cold water,
and drain well.

Combine macaroni, carrot, and next 4 ingredients; toss gently. Combine yogurt, mayonnaise, celery seeds, salt, and pepper; stir well. Add to pasta
mixture, tossing gently to combine. Chill thoroughly. To serve, spoon pasta mixture onto individual
lettuce-lined salad plates. Yield: 4 servings.

PER SERVING: 335 CALORIES (17% FROM FAT)
FAT 6.4G (SATURATED FAT 1.2G)
PROTEIN 17.8G   CARBOHYDRATE 49.5G
CHOLESTEROL 20MG   SODIUM 428MG

Sea Shell Salad

Grilled Tuna Niçoise

GRILLED TUNA NIÇOISE

¼ cup red wine vinegar
1½ tablespoons water
1 tablespoon Dijon mustard
2 teaspoons olive oil, divided
¾ pound fresh green beans
12 small round red potatoes
1 cup thinly sliced sweet red pepper
½ cup thinly sliced purple onion
¼ cup chopped fresh parsley
2 (8-ounce) tuna steaks
Vegetable cooking spray
6 cups torn fresh spinach
1½ cups yellow teardrop tomatoes, halved
2 hard-cooked eggs, sliced
6 Niçoise olives

Combine vinegar, water, mustard, and 1 teaspoon oil in a small jar. Cover and shake to blend.

Wash beans; trim ends, and remove strings. Arrange beans in a vegetable steamer over boiling water. Cover and steam 6 to 8 minutes or until crisp-tender. Drain; let cool slightly, and cut in half.

Arrange potatoes in a vegetable steamer over boiling water. Cover and steam 10 to 12 minutes or until tender. Drain. Let cool; cut into quarters.

Combine green beans, potato, red pepper, onion, and parsley; toss gently. Add vinegar mixture; toss gently. Cover and chill 2 hours.

Brush tuna with remaining 1 teaspoon olive oil. Coat grill rack with cooking spray; place on grill over hot coals (400° to 500°). Place tuna on rack; grill, covered, 5 minutes on each side or until fish flakes easily when tested with a fork. Remove tuna from grill; cut into ¼-inch-thick slices. Set aside; keep warm.

Place 1 cup spinach on each chilled salad plate;

top evenly with green bean mixture. Arrange tuna, tomato, egg, and olives evenly over green bean mixture. Yield: 6 servings.

PER SERVING: 270 CALORIES (27% FROM FAT)
FAT 8.0G (SATURATED FAT 1.8G)
PROTEIN 25.0G   CARBOHYDRATE 26.1G
CHOLESTEROL 99MG   SODIUM 195MG

WARM SHRIMP AND BLUE CHEESE PASTA SALAD

1½ quarts water
1 pound medium-size fresh shrimp, unpeeled
2 cups broccoli flowerets
3 cups uncooked tri-color rotini (corkscrew pasta)
2 cloves garlic, minced
2 teaspoons olive oil
1 medium-size sweet red or green pepper, cut into thin strips
½ cup coarsely crumbled blue cheese
½ cup chopped onion
⅛ teaspoon pepper

Bring water to a boil in a large Dutch oven. Add shrimp, and cook 3 to 5 minutes or until shrimp turns pink. Drain well; rinse with cold water, and cool slightly. Peel and devein shrimp; set aside.

Arrange broccoli in a vegetable steamer over boiling water. Cover and steam 2 minutes or until crisp-tender; set aside.

Cook pasta according to package directions, omitting salt and fat. Drain well and set aside.

Sauté garlic in oil in a large skillet over medium heat 1 minute. Add sweet red pepper, and sauté 2 minutes or until crisp-tender. Remove from heat; add shrimp, broccoli, pasta, and remaining ingredients, tossing gently. Serve warm. Yield: 4 (2-cup) servings.

PER SERVING: 348 CALORIES (21% FROM FAT)
FAT 8.2G (SATURATED FAT 3.3G)
PROTEIN 25.4G   CARBOHYDRATE 43.5G
CHOLESTEROL 135MG   SODIUM 366MG

SEAFOOD PAELLA SALAD

3 cups water
½ teaspoon salt
1½ cups uncooked long grain rice
½ teaspoon dried saffron
¾ cup water
¼ cup lemon juice
1 tablespoon olive oil
½ teaspoon chicken-flavored bouillon granules
¼ teaspoon salt
⅛ teaspoon black pepper
Dash of ground red pepper
4 cups water
¾ pound unpeeled small fresh shrimp
1 (9-ounce) package frozen artichoke hearts, thawed
¾ cup diced green pepper
½ cup frozen English peas, thawed
½ cup peeled, seeded, and chopped tomato
1 (4-ounce) jar diced pimiento, drained
1 tablespoon minced fresh parsley
Lettuce leaves

Bring 3 cups water and ½ teaspoon salt to a boil in a medium saucepan; stir in rice and saffron. Cover, reduce heat, and simmer 20 minutes or until rice is tender and liquid is absorbed.

Combine ¾ cup water and next 6 ingredients. Stir with a wire whisk until well blended. Add ½ cup dressing mixture to warm rice; stir well to separate grains. Transfer rice to a large bowl, and cool completely.

Bring 4 cups water to a boil; add shrimp, and cook 3 to 5 minutes or until shrimp turn pink. Drain well; rinse with cold water, and drain again. Peel and devein shrimp.

Add shrimp, artichoke hearts, green pepper, peas, tomato, and pimiento to cooled rice mixture; toss gently. Pour remaining dressing over rice mixture, and toss gently to coat. Cover and refrigerate at least 1 hour, stirring occasionally. Serve over lettuce leaves, and sprinkle with parsley. Yield: 6 (1⅓-cup) servings.

PER SERVING: 280 CALORIES (13% FROM FAT)
FAT 4.0G (SATURATED FAT 0.7G)
PROTEIN 15.2G   CARBOHYDRATE 45.8G
CHOLESTEROL 72MG   SODIUM 541MG

PIZZA & SANDWICHES

*D*ay is done, but dinner isn't even started. Easy solution: pizza or sandwiches. Wait! Don't pick up the phone—takeout is *out* and homemade is *in*.

Best of all, these pizzas and sandwiches will stand alone as one-dish meals. You get carbohydrates from the crust or bread; vitamins and minerals from the pizza sauce, tomato, or green pepper; and protein from the cheese or meat. Add a fruit salad or dessert, and you've designed a speedy but complete meal. Simply turn the pages to find suggestions for making your own creations.

Mighty Hero (Recipe follows on page 56)

BASIC PIZZA CRUST

1 tablespoon sugar
1 package dry yeast
1 cup warm water (105° to 115°)
3 cups all-purpose flour, divided
¼ teaspoon salt
1 teaspoon olive oil
Vegetable cooking spray
1 tablespoon cornmeal

Dissolve sugar and yeast in 1 cup warm water in a large bowl; let stand 5 minutes. Stir in 2¾ cups flour, salt, and oil to form a soft dough.

Turn dough out onto a lightly floured surface. Knead until smooth and elastic (about 5 minutes); add enough of remaining flour, 1 tablespoon at a time, to prevent dough from sticking to hands.

Place dough in a bowl coated with cooking spray, turning dough to coat top. Cover dough, and let rise in a warm place (85°), free from drafts, 1 hour or until doubled in bulk.

Punch dough down, and divide in half. Roll each half of dough into a 12-inch circle on a lightly floured surface. Place dough on 2 (12-inch) pizza pans or baking sheets coated with cooking spray and each sprinkled with ½ tablespoon cornmeal. Crimp edges of dough with fingers to form a rim. Cover and let rise in a warm place (85°), free from drafts, 30 minutes. Top and bake according to recipe directions. Yield: 2 (12-inch) pizza crusts.

Note: Store half of dough in freezer up to 1 month, if desired. Let dough rise; punch down, and divide in half. Dust half with flour; wrap in plastic wrap, and store in a heavy-duty, zip-top plastic bag in freezer. To thaw, place dough in refrigerator 12 hours; bring to room temperature, and shape as desired.

PER PIZZA CRUST: 756 CALORIES (6% FROM FAT)
FAT 4.7G (SATURATED FAT 0.6G)
PROTEIN 21.1G   CARBOHYDRATE 154.0G
CHOLESTEROL 0MG   SODIUM 297MG

DEEP DISH BASIC PIZZA CRUST

Place dough into 2 (9-inch) cakepans coated with cooking spray and each sprinkled with ½ tablespoon of cornmeal. Top and bake according to recipe directions. Yield: 2 (9-inch) deep dish pizza crusts.

FRESH TOMATO, BASIL, AND CHEESE PIZZA

1 (12-inch) Basic Pizza Crust
2 teaspoons olive oil
½ cup freshly grated Parmesan cheese, divided
3 large ripe unpeeled tomatoes, cut into ¼-inch slices (about 1½ pounds)
6 cloves garlic, thinly sliced
¼ teaspoon salt
⅛ teaspoon pepper
¼ cup chopped fresh basil

Brush crust with olive oil. Sprinkle with ¼ cup cheese, leaving a ½-inch border. Arrange tomato over cheese, overlapping. Top with garlic, remaining ¼ cup cheese, salt, and pepper. Bake at 500° for 12 minutes on bottom rack of oven. Remove pizza to a cutting board; top with basil. Let stand 5 minutes before slicing. Yield: 4 servings.

PER SERVING: 308 CALORIES (23% FROM FAT)
FAT 7.8G (SATURATED FAT 2.9G)
PROTEIN 12.1G   CARBOHYDRATE 48.5G
CHOLESTEROL 10MG   SODIUM 464MG

Quick Tip

If you don't have time to make your own crust, begin with a commercial pizza crust, split French bread loaves, split English muffins, tortillas, or pita bread. For a quick sauce, try one of the commercial low-sodium, low-fat pizza sauces.

Fresh Tomato, Basil, and Cheese Pizza

DEEP DISH SPINACH AND RICOTTA PIZZA

1 teaspoon olive oil
1 cup chopped onion, divided
3 cloves garlic, minced
1 (15-ounce) can no-salt-added stewed
    tomatoes, undrained and chopped
⅓ cup Burgundy or other dry red wine
¼ cup tomato paste
1 tablespoon red wine vinegar
½ teaspoon crushed red pepper
Vegetable cooking spray
4 cups coarsely chopped fresh spinach leaves
1 (15-ounce) carton low-fat ricotta cheese
¾ cup (3 ounces) shredded provolone cheese
¼ teaspoon ground black pepper
2 egg whites, lightly beaten
2 (9-inch) Deep Dish Basic Pizza Crusts
    (recipe on page 44)
¼ cup freshly grated Parmesan cheese

Heat oil in a large nonstick skillet over medium heat. Add ¾ cup onion and garlic; sauté 4 minutes. Add tomato and next 4 ingredients; bring to a boil. Reduce heat, and simmer, uncovered, 30 minutes or until reduced to 1½ cups, stirring occasionally.

Coat a large nonstick skillet with cooking spray; place over medium-high heat until hot. Add remaining ¼ cup onion, and sauté 3 minutes. Add spinach; sauté 1 minute. Squeeze spinach mixture on paper towels. Combine spinach mixture, ricotta cheese, and next 3 ingredients in a bowl; stir well.

Spread about 1⅓ cups ricotta mixture over each crust; top each with ¾ cup tomato sauce. Bake at 475° for 15 minutes. Sprinkle evenly with Parmesan cheese; bake 10 minutes. Yield: 8 servings.

PER SERVING: 326 CALORIES (21% FROM FAT)
FAT 7.6G (SATURATED FAT 3.8G)
PROTEIN 17.8G   CARBOHYDRATE 49.2G
CHOLESTEROL 17MG   SODIUM 314MG

Deep Dish Spinach and Ricotta Pizza

Mexican Black Bean Pizza

1 (15-ounce) can black beans, drained
⅓ cup diced purple onion
1 teaspoon ground cumin
1 teaspoon chili powder
⅛ teaspoon salt
1 clove garlic, minced
1 (12-inch) Basic Pizza Crust (recipe on
    page 44)
2½ cups unpeeled finely chopped tomato
    (about 2 large)
½ cup chopped green onions
3 tablespoons chopped fresh cilantro
1 tablespoon minced jalapeño pepper
½ cup (2 ounces) shredded Monterey Jack
    cheese
½ cup (2 ounces) shredded reduced-fat sharp
    Cheddar cheese

Place black beans in a bowl; partially mash until chunky. Add onion and next 4 ingredients; stir well. Spread evenly over prepared crust, leaving a ½-inch border.

Combine tomato and next 3 ingredients in a bowl; stir well. Sprinkle over bean mixture; top with cheeses. Bake at 500° for 12 to 15 minutes on bottom rack of oven. Remove pizza to a cutting board; let stand 5 minutes before slicing. Yield: 6 servings.

PER SERVING: 309 CALORIES (19% FROM FAT)
FAT 6.4G (SATURATED FAT 3.1G)
PROTEIN 16.0G   CARBOHYDRATE 48.6G
CHOLESTEROL 14MG   SODIUM 422MG

Whole Wheat Pizza Crust

1 tablespoon honey
1 package dry yeast
1 cup warm water (105° to 115°)
2 cups whole wheat flour, divided
1 cup all-purpose flour
¼ teaspoon salt
1 teaspoon olive oil
Vegetable cooking spray
1 tablespoon cornmeal

Dissolve honey and yeast in 1 cup warm water in a large bowl; let stand 5 minutes. Stir in 1¾ cups whole wheat flour and next 3 ingredients to form a soft dough.

Turn dough out onto a lightly floured surface. Knead until smooth and elastic (about 5 minutes); add enough of remaining flour, 1 tablespoon at a time, to prevent dough from sticking to hands.

Place dough in a bowl coated with cooking spray, turning to coat top. Cover dough, and let rise in a warm place (85°), free from drafts, 1 hour or until doubled in bulk.

Punch dough down; divide in half. Roll each half into a 12-inch circle on lightly floured surface. Place dough on 12-inch pizza pans or baking sheets coated with cooking spray and each sprinkled with ½ tablespoon cornmeal. Crimp edges of dough with fingers to form a rim. Cover and let rise in warm place (85°), free from drafts, 30 minutes. Top and bake according to recipe directions. Yield: 2 (12-inch) pizza crusts.

Note: Store half of dough in freezer up to 1 month, if desired. Let dough rise; punch down, and divide in half. Dust half with flour; wrap in plastic wrap, and store in a heavy-duty, zip-top plastic bag in freezer. To thaw, place dough in refrigerator 12 hours; bring to room temperature, and shape as desired.

PER PIZZA CRUST: 714 CALORIES (7% FROM FAT)
FAT 5.7G (SATURATED FAT 0.8G)
PROTEIN 24.6G   CARBOHYDRATE 147.8G
CHOLESTEROL 0MG   SODIUM 302MG

BEEF AND VEGETABLE PIZZA

1 pound 93% ultra-lean ground beef
½ cup chopped onion
2 cloves garlic, minced
¼ cup tomato paste
1 teaspoon dried basil
1 teaspoon dried oregano
½ teaspoon salt
¼ teaspoon crushed red pepper
1 (8-ounce) can no-salt-added tomato sauce
2 (12-inch) Whole Wheat Pizza Crusts (recipe on page 47)
6 small ripe unpeeled plum tomatoes, thinly sliced (about 1 pound)
2 large green peppers, cut into ¼-inch rings
1½ cups sliced fresh mushrooms
4 cloves garlic, thinly sliced
¾ cup (3 ounces) shredded part-skim mozzarella cheese

Cook beef, onion, and minced garlic in a large nonstick skillet over medium heat until browned, stirring to crumble. Drain and pat dry with paper towels. Return beef mixture to skillet; add tomato paste and next 5 ingredients, stirring well. Cook over medium-low heat 4 minutes or until thoroughly heated, stirring occasionally.

Spread 1¼ cups of beef mixture over each Whole Wheat Pizza Crust, leaving a ½-inch border; top with tomato and remaining ingredients. Bake at 450° for 14 minutes or until cheese melts. Remove to a cutting board; let stand 5 minutes before slicing. Yield: 8 servings.

PER SERVING: 345 CALORIES (20% FROM FAT)
FAT 7.5G (SATURATED FAT 2.7G)
PROTEIN 20.9G CARBOHYDRATE 51.1G
CHOLESTEROL 42MG SODIUM 408MG

VEGETARIAN PIZZAS

Vegetable cooking spray
3 tablespoons chopped purple onion
1 clove garlic, minced
½ cup sliced fresh mushrooms
⅓ cup coarsely shredded carrot
1 tablespoon minced fresh cilantro
2 (6-inch) flour tortillas
¾ cup (3 ounces) shredded part-skim mozzarella cheese, divided
½ cup canned kidney beans, drained

Coat a medium nonstick skillet with cooking spray; place over medium heat until hot. Add onion and garlic; sauté 1 minute. Add mushrooms and carrot; sauté 2 minutes. Stir in cilantro; set aside.

Place tortillas on a baking sheet, and broil 6 inches from heat 2 minutes. Turn tortillas over; broil 1 minute or until crisp.

Remove from oven; top each tortilla with ¼ cup plus 1 tablespoon cheese, ¼ cup beans, half of mushroom mixture, and 1 tablespoon remaining cheese. Broil 6 inches from heat 1 minute or until cheese melts. Yield: 2 servings.

PER SERVING: 298 CALORIES (30% FROM FAT)
FAT 9.9G (SATURATED FAT 4.7G)
PROTEIN 17.6G CARBOHYDRATE 34.8G
CHOLESTEROL 25MG SODIUM 597MG

Did You Know?

In Naples, where pizza is said to have originated, hungry peasant women would break off pieces of bread dough, flatten it, and top the dough with whatever seasonings were on hand. Tomatoes (once thought to be poisonous) were not added to those first pieces of dough. And not until 1889 was cheese even used: an Italian baker, commissioned to prepare pizza for a queen, added mozzarella to a tomato-and-basil pizza to salute the colors of the Italian flag.

Vegetarian Pizzas

GARDEN MEDLEY PIZZA WITH OATMEAL CRUST

(pictured on cover)

1 package dry yeast
¾ cup warm water (105° to 115°), divided
2 tablespoons honey
2 cups all-purpose flour
¾ cup regular oats, uncooked
½ teaspoon salt
Vegetable cooking spray
1 teaspoon vegetable oil
1 cup thinly sliced broccoli flowerets
1 cup thinly sliced broccoli stalks
½ cup diagonally sliced green onions
1 small green pepper, seeded and cut into
    strips
1 small sweet red pepper, seeded and cut into
    strips
2 cups sliced fresh mushrooms
1 medium-size yellow squash, sliced and
    quartered
1 (8-ounce) can no-salt-added tomato sauce
1 (6-ounce) can no-salt-added tomato paste
2 tablespoons red wine vinegar
¾ teaspoon dried basil
½ teaspoon dried oregano
3 cloves garlic, minced
1 cup (4 ounces) finely shredded part-skim
    mozzarella cheese
1 cup (4 ounces) finely shredded 40% less-fat
    Cheddar cheese

Dissolve yeast in ¼ cup warm water in a 1-cup liquid measuring cup; let stand 5 minutes. Stir in honey.

Combine flour, oats, and salt in a large bowl. Add yeast mixture and remaining ½ cup warm water to flour mixture, mixing well until a soft dough forms.

Turn dough out onto a lightly floured surface, and knead until smooth and elastic (about 8 to 10 minutes). Place dough in a bowl coated with cooking spray, turning to coat top. Cover and let rise in a warm place (85°), free from drafts, 1 hour or until doubled in bulk.

Coat a large nonstick skillet with cooking spray; add oil. Place over medium-high heat until hot.

Add broccoli flowerets and next 4 ingredients; sauté 3 minutes. Add mushrooms and squash, and sauté until mushrooms are tender. Set aside.

Combine tomato sauce and next 5 ingredients in a medium saucepan. Bring mixture to a boil, stirring constantly. Cover, reduce heat, and simmer 15 minutes.

Punch dough down. Press dough onto a 14-inch pizza pan coated with cooking spray. Spread tomato sauce mixture evenly over crust. Arrange vegetable mixture evenly over sauce. Bake at 425° for 20 minutes. Combine cheeses; sprinkle evenly over top of pizza, and bake an additional 5 minutes. Yield: 6 servings.

PER SERVING: 384 CALORIES (19% FROM FAT)
FAT 8.1G (SATURATED FAT 3.6G)
PROTEIN 19.8G   CARBOHYDRATE 59.9G
CHOLESTEROL 21MG   SODIUM 464MG

BROCCOLI AND CHEESE CALZONES

1 package dry yeast
1 cup warm water (105° to 115°), divided
1 tablespoon honey
1¾ cups whole wheat flour
1 cup unbleached flour
½ teaspoon salt
3 tablespoons whole wheat flour, divided
Vegetable cooking spray
3 cups chopped fresh broccoli flowerets
½ cup chopped onion
⅓ cup shredded carrot
⅓ cup commercial oil-free Italian dressing
¼ teaspoon freshly ground pepper
1½ cups (6 ounces) shredded part-skim
    mozzarella cheese
1 egg
1 tablespoon water
2 tablespoons freshly grated Parmesan cheese

Dissolve yeast in ¼ cup warm water in a large mixing bowl; let stand 5 minutes.

Combine remaining ¾ cup warm water and

Broccoli and Cheese Calzones

honey; add to yeast mixture, stirring gently. Gradually stir in 1¾ cups whole wheat flour, unbleached flour, and salt to make a soft dough.

Sprinkle 1 tablespoon whole wheat flour evenly over work surface. Turn dough out onto floured surface, and knead until smooth and elastic (about 8 to 10 minutes). Place dough in a large bowl that has been coated with cooking spray, turning to grease top. Cover dough and let rise in a warm place (85°), free from drafts, 45 minutes or until doubled in bulk.

Cook broccoli in boiling water 3 minutes or until crisp-tender. Drain; rinse with cold water, and drain again. Combine broccoli, onion, shredded carrot, and dressing in a small bowl.

Punch dough down, and divide into 6 equal portions. Shape each portion into a ball; cover and let rest 5 minutes. Sprinkle 1 teaspoon flour over work surface. Roll one portion into a 7-inch circle. Repeat with remaining portions, using 1 teaspoon whole wheat flour for each circle.

Divide broccoli mixture into 6 portions. Place one portion on half of each circle of dough. Sprinkle pepper and mozzarella cheese evenly over broccoli mixture. Combine egg and 1 tablespoon water; moisten edges of circles with egg mixture. Fold circles in half; crimp edges to seal. Sprinkle each with 1 teaspoon Parmesan cheese. Bake at 425° for 10 minutes or until golden brown. Yield: 6 servings.

PER SERVING: 335 CALORIES (19% FROM FAT)
FAT 7.2G (SATURATED FAT 3.7G)
PROTEIN 18.1G   CARBOHYDRATE 52.6G
CHOLESTEROL 55MG   SODIUM 537MG

Roast and Relish Sandwiches

ROAST AND RELISH SANDWICHES

You can lower the sodium of this sandwich by using thinly sliced unsalted roast beef instead of the deli meat that is pictured.

½ cup chopped red cabbage
¼ cup plus 2 tablespoons commercial corn
     relish
¼ cup finely chopped green onions
2 (2½-ounce) whole wheat submarine rolls,
     split
5 ounces thinly sliced lean, cooked roast beef

Combine first 3 ingredients in a bowl; stir well. Spoon half of cabbage mixture on each roll bottom; top with roast beef, and cover with roll tops. Yield: 2 servings.

PER SERVING: 352 CALORIES (27% FROM FAT)
FAT 10.6G (SATURATED FAT 3.4G)
PROTEIN 20.6G CARBOHYDRATE 44.9G
CHOLESTEROL 21MG SODIUM 1011MG

SMOTHERED BEEF AND MUSHROOMS

1 (⅞-ounce) package dried porcini mushrooms
1 cup hot water
1 pound lean boneless top round steak
Vegetable cooking spray
1 pound small fresh mushrooms, halved
½ teaspoon dried marjoram
3 cloves garlic, minced
1 cup dry Marsala
1 tablespoon no-salt-added tomato paste
¼ teaspoon salt
¼ teaspoon pepper
2 teaspoons all-purpose flour
2 tablespoons water
8 (½-inch-thick) slices French bread, toasted

Combine dried porcini mushrooms and 1 cup hot water in a small bowl; let stand 15 minutes. Drain, reserving liquid. Coarsely chop porcini mushrooms, and set aside.

Partially freeze steak; trim fat from steak. Slice steak diagonally across grain into ¼-inch-wide strips; cut strips into 2-inch pieces. Coat a large nonstick skillet with cooking spray; place over medium-high heat until hot. Add steak, and cook 5 minutes or until browned on all sides. Remove steak from skillet. Drain and pat dry with paper towels. Wipe drippings from skillet with a paper towel.

Coat skillet with cooking spray. Add porcini mushrooms, halved mushrooms, marjoram, and minced garlic; sauté until tender. Return steak to skillet. Add reserved mushroom liquid, Marsala, and next 3 ingredients; stir well. Bring mixture to a boil; cover, reduce heat, and simmer 30 minutes or until steak is tender.

Combine flour and 2 tablespoons water, stirring until smooth. Add to steak mixture, and stir well. Cook over medium heat, stirring constantly, until mixture is thickened.

To serve, place 2 slices French bread on each individual serving plate; spoon beef mixture evenly over bread. Serve immediately. Yield: 4 servings.

PER SERVING: 337 CALORIES (19% FROM FAT)
FAT 7.1G (SATURATED FAT 2.1G)
PROTEIN 33.4G CARBOHYDRATE 33.0G
CHOLESTEROL 73MG SODIUM 402MG

Menu Helper

To take the boredom out of building a sandwich, try a different bread in place of the usual sliced white or wheat bread. Bagels, rolls, English muffins, pita bread, and raisin bread add delightful new textures. Then match up the old standbys—ham, turkey, chicken, and roast beef—with chutney, relishes, or flavored mustards.

HEARTY MEATBALL SUBS

6 (2½-ounce) submarine rolls, unsplit
1 pound ground round
2 (8-ounce) cans no-salt-added tomato sauce,
     divided
¼ cup seasoned breadcrumbs
¼ cup minced onion
¼ teaspoon salt
1 clove garlic, minced
Vegetable cooking spray
2 teaspoons olive oil
1½ cups (1½-inch) julienne-sliced green
     pepper
1 cup slivered onion
2 tablespoons tomato paste
½ teaspoon dried basil

   Slanting knife at an angle, cut a 5- x 1½-inch oval piece out of top of each roll. Scoop out roll, leaving a 1½-inch-wide cavity. Set rolls aside; reserve remaining bread for another use.

   Combine ground round, ¼ cup tomato sauce, and next 4 ingredients in a bowl; stir well. Shape into 54 (1-inch) meatballs; place on a rack coated with cooking spray. Place rack in a roasting pan. Bake at 350° for 15 minutes or until done.

   Coat a nonstick skillet with cooking spray; add oil. Place over medium heat until hot. Add green pepper and onion; sauté 5 minutes. Add remaining tomato sauce, tomato paste, and basil; simmer, uncovered, 5 minutes. Add meatballs, stirring gently to coat; cook 3 minutes or until heated. Spoon 9 meatballs into each roll; divide sauce evenly. Yield: 6 servings.

PER SERVING: 339 CALORIES (20% FROM FAT)
FAT 7.6G (SATURATED FAT 2.3G)
PROTEIN 23.0G   CARBOHYDRATE 42.6G
CHOLESTEROL 48MG   SODIUM 576MG

Hearty Meatball Sub

BUFFALO CHICKEN SANDWICH

2 cups thinly sliced cabbage
¼ cup minced radish
3 tablespoons plain nonfat yogurt
1 tablespoon reduced-calorie mayonnaise
4 (4-ounce) skinned, boned chicken breast
   halves
2 tablespoons hot sauce
2 tablespoons water
Vegetable cooking spray
2 ounces blue cheese, crumbled
4 (2-ounce) kaiser rolls, split and toasted

Combine first 4 ingredients in a medium bowl; toss gently. Cover and chill at least 30 minutes.

Place chicken between 2 sheets of heavy-duty plastic wrap, and flatten to ¼-inch thickness, using a meat mallet or rolling pin. Place chicken in a heavy-duty, zip-top plastic bag.

Combine hot sauce and water; pour over chicken. Marinate in refrigerator 15 minutes. Remove chicken from plastic bag, and discard hot sauce mixture.

Coat a large nonstick skillet with cooking spray; place over medium-high heat until hot. Add chicken, and cook 5 minutes on each side or until lightly browned. Remove chicken from skillet; drain and pat dry with paper towels. Wipe drippings from skillet with a paper towel.

Return chicken to skillet; sprinkle with blue cheese. Cover and cook over low heat until cheese melts. Place a chicken breast half on bottom half of a kaiser roll; spoon ½ cup cabbage mixture over chicken. Top with remaining half of roll. Repeat procedure with remaining rolls, chicken, and cabbage mixture. Yield: 4 servings.

PER SERVING: 405 CALORIES (23% FROM FAT)
FAT 10.3G (SATURATED FAT 3.7G)
PROTEIN 38.0G   CARBOHYDRATE 40.9G
CHOLESTEROL 82MG   SODIUM 854MG

GREEK CHICKEN SANDWICHES

To help keep these sandwiches rolled for easy eating, wrap the rolled lower half of each in plastic wrap or wax paper.

½ cup skim milk
½ cup Italian-seasoned breadcrumbs
1 pound skinned, boned chicken breast, cut
   into ¼-inch-wide strips
Vegetable cooking spray
1 tablespoon vegetable oil
6 romaine lettuce leaves
6 (¼-inch-thick) slices unpeeled tomato, each
   cut in half
6 (⅛-inch-thick) slices green pepper, each cut
   in half
6 (7-inch) pita bread rounds, uncut
¾ cup commercial reduced-calorie Ranch
   dressing

Place milk in a large bowl; set aside. Place breadcrumbs in a large zip-top plastic bag. Add chicken to milk; stir well, and drain. Add chicken to plastic bag with breadcrumbs; seal bag, and shake to coat chicken with breadcrumbs.

Coat a large nonstick skillet with cooking spray; add oil, and place over medium-high heat until hot. Add chicken, and sauté 7 minutes or until done. Set aside.

Arrange 1 lettuce leaf, 2 pieces tomato, and 2 pieces green pepper down the center of each pita bread round, and top each with 2 ounces chicken. Drizzle 2 tablespoons dressing over each sandwich, and roll up. Yield: 6 servings.

PER SERVING: 310 CALORIES (29% FROM FAT)
FAT 10.1G (SATURATED FAT 1.9G)
PROTEIN 19.9G   CARBOHYDRATE 34.0G
CHOLESTEROL 42MG   SODIUM 839MG

MIGHTY HERO

(pictured on page 42)

Serve this sandwich with a glass of skim milk and a piece of fresh fruit for a complete, nutritious meal.

1 (16-ounce) round loaf sourdough bread
¼ cup balsamic vinegar
1 tablespoon olive oil
1 teaspoon dried oregano
1 teaspoon dried parsley flakes
¼ teaspoon pepper
2 cloves garlic, minced
1 cup sliced fresh mushrooms
6 (¼-inch-thick) slices tomato
2 (¼-inch-thick) slices purple onion, separated into rings
2 cups shredded zucchini
8 (1-ounce) slices lean turkey
6 (1-ounce) slices part-skim mozzarella cheese

Slice bread in half horizontally, using an electric or serrated knife. Carefully remove soft bread from inside each half, leaving ½-inch-thick shells. Set aside; reserve soft bread for another use.

Combine vinegar and next 5 ingredients in a shallow baking dish; add mushrooms, tomato, and onion. Let stand 15 to 20 minutes.

Drain with a slotted spoon, reserving marinade. Brush marinade evenly inside each bread cavity. Spoon 1 cup zucchini into bottom half; arrange half of mushroom mixture over zucchini. Layer with 4 turkey slices and 3 cheese slices. Repeat layers with remaining zucchini, mushroom mixture, turkey, and cheese. Top with remaining half of loaf. Wrap loaf securely in heavy-duty aluminum foil; chill until ready to serve. To serve, unwrap and slice loaf into wedges. Yield: 6 servings.

PER SERVING: 303 CALORIES (28% FROM FAT)
FAT 9.4G (SATURATED FAT 3.6G)
PROTEIN 24.5G   CARBOHYDRATE 31.0G
CHOLESTEROL 43MG   SODIUM 437MG

TURKEY-PIMIENTO SANDWICHES

1 (2-ounce) jar sliced pimiento
¾ teaspoon extra-spicy salt-free herb and spice blend, divided
2 (2½-ounce) turkey breast cutlets
Vegetable cooking spray
4 (1-ounce) slices pumpernickel bread
⅔ cup alfalfa sprouts
10 thin slices unpeeled cucumber

Position knife blade in food processor bowl; add pimiento and ¼ teaspoon spice blend. Process 1 minute or until smooth, and set aside. Sprinkle both sides of cutlets with remaining ½ teaspoon spice blend.

Coat a skillet with cooking spray, and place over medium heat until hot. Add cutlets, and cook about 2 minutes on each side or until done; set aside. Spread pimiento puree over 2 bread slices; top each with half of alfalfa sprouts, 1 cutlet, 5 cucumber slices, and remaining bread. Yield: 2 servings.

PER SERVING: 241 CALORIES (6% FROM FAT)
FAT 1.7G (SATURATED FAT 0.3G)
PROTEIN 22.6G   CARBOHYDRATE 35.7G
CHOLESTEROL 45MG   SODIUM 364MG

LAMB BURGERS

3 tablespoons plain nonfat yogurt
1 tablespoon nonfat mayonnaise
½ teaspoon prepared mustard
¼ teaspoon paprika
1 pound lean ground lamb
½ teaspoon garlic powder
½ teaspoon dried oregano
½ teaspoon low-sodium Worcestershire sauce
¼ teaspoon paprika
¼ teaspoon pepper
Vegetable cooking spray
4 lettuce leaves
4 tomato slices
4 onion rolls, split and toasted

Combine first 4 ingredients. Cover and chill.

Combine lamb and next 5 ingredients, stirring well; shape into 4 (¼-inch-thick) patties. Place on rack of a broiler pan coated with cooking spray. Broil 3 inches from heat (with electric oven door partially opened) 3 to 4 minutes on each side or to desired degree of doneness. Drain on paper towels.

Place a lettuce leaf, tomato slice, and lamb patty on bottom of each bun half. Top each with 1 tablespoon yogurt mixture and remaining bun halves. Yield: 4 servings.

PER SERVING: 343 CALORIES (25% FROM FAT)
FAT 9.6G (SATURATED FAT 3.1G)
PROTEIN 29.0G   CARBOHYDRATE 33.6G
CHOLESTEROL 80MG   SODIUM 293MG

MOCK GYROS

½ cup chopped cucumber
½ cup nonfat sour cream
¼ cup plain nonfat yogurt
1 teaspoon olive oil
1 pound lean ground lamb
1 teaspoon dried oregano
½ teaspoon dried thyme
¼ teaspoon salt
1 tablespoon lemon juice
2 (6-inch) pita bread rounds, cut in half crosswise
1 cup thinly sliced onion
1½ cups shredded lettuce

Combine first 3 ingredients in a small bowl; stir well. Cover and chill 30 minutes.

Heat oil in a large nonstick skillet over medium heat. Add lamb, oregano, thyme, and salt; cook until browned, stirring to crumble. Drain; pat dry with paper towels. Add lemon juice to lamb; toss.

Spoon lamb mixture evenly into pita halves. Top evenly with onion and lettuce. Serve with sour cream mixture. Yield: 4 servings.

PER SERVING: 328 CALORIES (28% FROM FAT)
FAT 10.3G (SATURATED FAT 3.2G)
PROTEIN 31.9G   CARBOHYDRATE 24.3G
CHOLESTEROL 100MG   SODIUM 443MG

OPEN-FACED SESAME PORK SANDWICHES

1 clove garlic, minced
2 (4-ounce) boneless pork cutlets, tenderized
1 teaspoon sesame seeds
Vegetable cooking spray
1 cup sliced fresh mushrooms
½ cup thinly sliced onion
2 tablespoons commercial Major Grey chutney
2 teaspoons Dijon mustard
1 whole wheat English muffin, split and toasted

Rub minced garlic over both sides of pork cutlets; sprinkle both sides evenly with sesame seeds. Coat a medium skillet with cooking spray, and place over medium heat until hot. Add cutlets; cook 4 minutes on each side or until done. Remove cutlets from skillet; set aside, and keep warm. Wipe drippings from skillet with a paper towel.

Recoat pan with cooking spray, and place over medium heat until hot. Add mushrooms and onion; sauté 3 minutes. Stir in chutney and Dijon mustard; cook 30 seconds or until thoroughly heated. Place each cutlet on 1 English muffin half; top with half of mushroom mixture. Yield: 2 servings.

Note: Ask your butcher to tenderize the pork cutlets using a tenderizing machine.

PER SERVING: 309 CALORIES (19% FROM FAT)
FAT 6.4G (SATURATED FAT 1.6G)
PROTEIN 28.7G   CARBOHYDRATE 33.1G
CHOLESTEROL 79MG   SODIUM 409MG

Fat Alert

Hold the mayo—at least the fattening kind. Nonfat yogurt, nonfat mayonnaise, and mustard reduce fat significantly in the Lamb Burgers; Dijon mustard and chutney complement the pork in Open-Faced Sesame Pork Sandwiches.

Pork and Slaw Sandwiches

PORK AND SLAW SANDWICHES

1   pound lean ground pork
½ cup chopped onion
1 (8-ounce) can no-salt-added tomato sauce
1 tablespoon brown sugar
1 tablespoon low-sodium Worcestershire sauce
1 teaspoon dry mustard
1 teaspoon liquid smoke
½ teaspoon pepper
1½ cups finely shredded red cabbage
½ cup finely chopped Granny Smith apple
½ cup finely shredded carrot
½ cup pineapple low-fat yogurt
¾ teaspoon curry powder
½ teaspoon dry mustard
6 reduced-calorie whole wheat hamburger
    buns, split

Cook pork and onion in a nonstick skillet over medium heat until pork is browned, stirring to crumble. Drain and pat dry with paper towels. Wipe drippings from skillet with a paper towel.

Return pork mixture to skillet; add tomato sauce and next 5 ingredients. Bring to a boil; cover, reduce heat, and simmer 15 minutes, stirring occasionally. Set aside, and keep warm.

Combine cabbage and next 5 ingredients in a bowl; stir well. Spoon pork mixture onto bottom halves of buns; top with cabbage mixture. Top with bun halves. Serve immediately. Yield: 6 servings.

PER SERVING: 289 CALORIES (32% FROM FAT)
FAT 10.3G (SATURATED FAT 3.7G)
PROTEIN 19.7G   CARBOHYDRATE 28.4G
CHOLESTEROL 55MG   SODIUM 296MG

CATFISH PO-BOYS

Vegetable cooking spray
¼ cup chopped onion
2 tablespoons chopped green pepper
2 tablespoons chopped celery
½ cup seeded, chopped tomato
2 tablespoons minced fresh parsley
½ teaspoon garlic powder
¼ cup plus 1 tablespoon plain nonfat yogurt
3 tablespoons nonfat mayonnaise
¼ teaspoon hot sauce
½ cup crushed corn flakes cereal
¾ teaspoon salt-free lemon-pepper seasoning
¾ teaspoon paprika
¾ pound farm-raised catfish fillets, cut into
   1-inch pieces
1 egg white, lightly beaten
1 cup shredded iceberg lettuce
4 reduced-calorie whole wheat buns

Coat a large nonstick skillet with cooking spray; place over medium-high heat until hot. Add onion, green pepper, and celery; sauté until tender. Stir in tomato, parsley, and garlic powder. Transfer mixture to a bowl; let cool slightly. Stir in yogurt, mayonnaise, and hot sauce. Cover and chill thoroughly.

Combine cereal, lemon-pepper seasoning, and paprika. Dip fish pieces in egg white; dredge in cereal mixture. Place on a baking sheet coated with cooking spray. Bake at 500° for 4 minutes. Turn fish, and bake 4 minutes or until crisp and golden.

Place ¼ cup lettuce on bottom half of each bun. Top with fish pieces. Spoon yogurt mixture over fish. Top with bun halves. Serve immediately. Yield: 4 servings.

PER SERVING: 256 CALORIES (18% FROM FAT)
FAT 5.1G (SATURATED FAT 0.9G)
PROTEIN 20.9G   CARBOHYDRATE 30.2G
CHOLESTEROL 50MG   SODIUM 563MG

LEMON-BASIL TUNA POCKETS

2 (6⅛-ounce) cans 60% less-salt tuna packed
   in spring water, drained
½ cup chopped celery
¼ cup sliced green onions
2 tablespoons chopped fresh basil
2 tablespoons commercial oil-free Italian
   dressing
2 tablespoons lemon juice
1 tablespoon water
¼ teaspoon salt-free lemon-pepper seasoning
1 clove garlic, minced
6 green leaf lettuce leaves
6 (¼-inch-thick) slices tomato
3 (6-inch) whole wheat pita bread rounds, cut
   in half crosswise

Combine first 3 ingredients in a bowl; stir well. Combine basil and next 5 ingredients; stir well. Pour over tuna mixture; stir well. Cover and refrigerate at least 1 hour.

Just before serving, place 1 lettuce leaf and 1 tomato slice in each pita half; spoon tuna mixture into pitas. Yield: 3 servings.

PER SERVING: 282 CALORIES (7% FROM FAT)
FAT 2.2G (SATURATED FAT 0.4G)
PROTEIN 28.0G   CARBOHYDRATE 34.0G
CHOLESTEROL 28MG   SODIUM 400MG

Lighten Up

Whether eating at a restaurant or at home, avoid sandwiches made with high-fat meats: corned beef, bologna, meatballs, pastrami, sausage, luncheon meats, and meat loaf. Order a turkey, chicken, or fish sandwich instead, and ask the cook to go easy on the mayonnaise and cheese.

STEWS & SUCH

*B*r-r-r! Old Man Winter may put a nip in the air, but you can minimize his bluster. On a cold winter day, nothing satisfies like a bowl of hearty stew or soup. These recipes are loaded with vegetables, starches, and protein.

As with other one-dish recipes, we recommend a bread or salad on the side to satisfy heartier appetites. Suggested breads include naturally low-fat French or Italian bread, bagels, breadsticks, toasted pita bread, or warm flour tortillas. With lighter soups, crackers are always an option.

Mexican Meatball Stew (Recipe follows on page 63)

ACORN SQUASH-BEEF STEW

1½ pounds lean boneless round steak (½ inch thick)
Vegetable cooking spray
2½ cups water
1 medium onion, sliced
2 stalks celery, cut into ½-inch slices
2 tablespoons dry sherry
2 teaspoons beef-flavored bouillon granules
½ teaspoon ground coriander
½ teaspoon ground cumin
½ teaspoon ground ginger
¼ teaspoon ground red pepper
2 cups cubed acorn squash (about 1 medium)
1 (15½-ounce) can red kidney beans, drained
2 tablespoons chopped fresh parsley

Trim fat from steak; cut steak into 1-inch pieces. Coat a Dutch oven with cooking spray; place over medium-high heat until hot. Add steak; cook until browned on all sides, stirring frequently. Drain and pat dry with paper towels. Wipe pan drippings from pan with a paper towel.

Return meat to pan; add water and next 8 ingredients. Bring to a boil; cover, reduce heat, and simmer 1½ hours. Add squash and beans; cook, covered, an additional 10 minutes or until meat and squash are tender. Ladle stew into individual bowls, and sprinkle ½ tablespoon parsley over each serving. Yield: 4 (1½-cup) servings.

PER SERVING: 361 CALORIES (23% FROM FAT)
FAT 9.1G (SATURATED FAT 3.1G)
PROTEIN 47.7G   CARBOHYDRATE 20.0G
CHOLESTEROL 110MG   SODIUM 693MG

Acorn Squash-Beef Stew

CHUCK WAGON STEW

Round steak is recommended here, but you can also use about ³/₄ pound leftover cooked roast beef or pork.

1 pound lean boneless round steak (½ inch thick)
Vegetable cooking spray
2 cups coarsely chopped carrot
1 medium onion, cut into eighths
2¼ cups cubed red potato
1 (14½-ounce) can no-salt-added whole tomatoes, undrained and chopped
1 cup water
1 cup brewed coffee
2 tablespoons molasses
1 tablespoon low-sodium Worcestershire sauce
1 teaspoon beef-flavored bouillon granules
½ teaspoon dried thyme
½ teaspoon dried marjoram
¼ teaspoon hot sauce
1 bay leaf
1 (15-ounce) can pinto beans, undrained

Trim fat from steak; cut steak into 1-inch pieces. Coat a Dutch oven with cooking spray; place over medium-high heat until hot. Add steak; cook until browned on all sides, stirring frequently. Drain and pat dry with paper towels. Wipe drippings from pan with a paper towel.

Coat pan with cooking spray; place over medium-high heat until hot. Add carrot and onion; sauté until carrot is lightly browned. Return steak to pan. Add potato and next 10 ingredients, stirring well to combine. Bring to a boil; cover, reduce heat, and simmer 1 hour and 15 minutes or until potato and steak are tender.

Add pinto beans, and stir well. Cover and simmer an additional 15 minutes. Remove and discard bay leaf. Yield: 6 (1²/₃-cup) servings.

PER SERVING: 256 CALORIES (15% FROM FAT)
FAT 4.2G (SATURATED FAT 1.3G)
PROTEIN 20.9G   CARBOHYDRATE 34.3G
CHOLESTEROL 40MG   SODIUM 530MG

MEXICAN MEATBALL STEW

(pictured on page 60)

1 pound ground round
¼ cup soft breadcrumbs
1 egg, lightly beaten
1 (4-ounce) can chopped green chiles, drained and divided
½ teaspoon ground cumin
¼ teaspoon pepper
Vegetable cooking spray
⅓ cup all-purpose flour
2¼ cups water
1 cup frozen whole kernel corn
1 (14½-ounce) can no-salt-added whole tomatoes, undrained and chopped
1 (15-ounce) can kidney beans, drained
1 tablespoon chili powder
1 teaspoon beef-flavored bouillon granules
1 teaspoon dried oregano

Combine ground round, breadcrumbs, egg, 3 tablespoons chiles, cumin, and pepper in a medium bowl; stir well. Shape mixture into meatballs, using about 2 teaspoons mixture for each meatball. Arrange meatballs on rack of a broiler pan coated with cooking spray. Broil 5½ inches from heat 5 minutes; turn meatballs, and broil an additional 4 minutes or until browned. Drain and pat dry with paper towels.

Combine flour and water in a Dutch oven; stir well. Cook over medium heat until thickened and bubbly. Add meatballs, remaining chiles, corn, and remaining ingredients. Bring to a boil; cover, reduce heat, and simmer 30 minutes. Yield: 5 (1½-cup) servings.

PER SERVING: 318 CALORIES (22% FROM FAT)
FAT 7.6G (SATURATED FAT 2.5G)
PROTEIN 29.4G   CARBOHYDRATE 34.2G
CHOLESTEROL 100MG   SODIUM 307MG

Beef Stew with Burgundy

BEEF STEW WITH BURGUNDY

1½ pounds lean, boneless round steak
1 teaspoon vegetable oil
½ teaspoon dried thyme
2 large cloves garlic, minced
2 bay leaves
3 cups Burgundy or other dry red wine
¼ cup tomato paste
½ cup plus 3 tablespoons water, divided
2½ cups quartered fresh mushrooms (about ½ pound)
12 small round red potatoes, peeled and quartered (about 1½ pounds)
6 medium carrots, cut into 1-inch pieces
2 small onions, quartered (about ½ pound)
2 (10½-ounce) cans low-sodium chicken broth
3 tablespoons cornstarch
¼ cup chopped fresh parsley
1 teaspoon salt
¼ teaspoon pepper

Trim fat from steak. Cut steak into 1-inch cubes. Heat oil in a large Dutch oven over high heat until hot. Add steak; cook 5 minutes or until steak loses its pink color. Drain well. Wipe drippings from pan with a paper towel.

Return steak to pan; place over medium heat. Add thyme, garlic, and bay leaves; cook 1 minute. Add wine and tomato paste; bring to a boil. Cover, reduce heat, and simmer 1½ hours or until steak is tender. Add ½ cup water and next 5 ingredients; bring to a boil. Cover, reduce heat, and simmer 40 minutes or until vegetables are tender.

Combine cornstarch and remaining 3 tablespoons water; add to stew. Cook 2 minutes or until thickened, stirring constantly. Stir in parsley, salt, and pepper. Remove and discard bay leaves. Yield: 6 (1⅔-cup) servings.

Note: Store stew in an airtight container in freezer up to 3 months, if desired. Thaw in refrigerator; reheat to serve.

PER SERVING: 367 CALORIES (18% FROM FAT)
FAT 7.5G (SATURATED FAT 2.5G)
PROTEIN 33.8G CARBOHYDRATE 42.2G
CHOLESTEROL 73MG SODIUM 531MG

NONALCOHOLIC VERSION

Instead of 3 cups red wine, substitute 1 (13½-ounce) can no-salt-added beef broth, ¾ cup non-alcoholic red wine, ⅓ cup water, and ¼ cup red wine vinegar. Yield: 6 (1⅔-cup) servings.

PER SERVING: 376 CALORIES (18% FROM FAT)
FAT 7.4G (SATURATED FAT 2.1G)
PROTEIN 33.8G CARBOHYDRATE 43.0G
CHOLESTEROL 73MG SODIUM 527MG

LENTIL-LAMB STEW

1 pound lean boneless leg of lamb
Vegetable cooking spray
7 cups water
2 cups dried lentils
1½ cups chopped tomato
1 cup diced onion
¾ cup diced carrot
¼ cup brown rice, uncooked
2 tablespoons fresh lemon juice
1 teaspoon dried oregano
½ teaspoon garlic powder
¼ teaspoon salt
1 cup shredded fresh spinach
Thin lemon slices (optional)

Trim fat from lamb; cut lamb into 1-inch pieces. Coat a Dutch oven with cooking spray; place over medium-high heat until hot. Add lamb, and cook 10 minutes or until lamb is browned on all sides, stirring occasionally. Drain and pat dry with paper towels. Wipe drippings from pan with a paper towel.

Return lamb to pan; add water and next 9 ingredients. Bring to a boil; cover, reduce heat, and simmer 1 hour or until lentils and lamb are tender. Stir in spinach; cook 1 minute. Ladle stew into individual bowls, and garnish with lemon slices, if desired. Yield: 8 (1¼-cup) servings.

PER SERVING: 287 CALORIES (13% FROM FAT)
FAT 4.2G (SATURATED FAT 1.3G)
PROTEIN 26.8G CARBOHYDRATE 36.6G
CHOLESTEROL 38MG SODIUM 119MG

Lamb Stew with White Beans and Tomatoes

1 pound lean ground lamb
1½ cups coarsely chopped onion
3 cloves garlic, minced
3 cups peeled, cubed baking potato (about 1 pound)
2 cups no-salt-added chicken broth, undiluted
1½ teaspoons dried rosemary, crushed
2 (14½-ounce) cans no-salt-added whole tomatoes, undrained and chopped
1 (15.8-ounce) can Great Northern beans, drained
½ teaspoon salt
½ teaspoon freshly ground pepper

Combine first 3 ingredients in a Dutch oven; cook over medium heat until lamb is browned, stirring to crumble. Remove mixture from pan. Drain and pat dry with paper towels; set aside.

Combine potato, broth, and rosemary in pan; bring to a boil. Cover, reduce heat to medium, and cook 15 minutes or until potato is tender. Return lamb mixture to pan. Stir in tomato, beans, salt, and pepper. Cook 5 minutes or until thoroughly heated. Yield: 6 (1½-cup) servings.

PER SERVING: 287 CALORIES (19% FROM FAT)
FAT 5.9G (SATURATED FAT 2.1G)
PROTEIN 24.2G   CARBOHYDRATE 34.2G
CHOLESTEROL 54MG   SODIUM 390MG

Cooking Tip

An enameled cast-iron Dutch oven is excellent for cooking stews, soups, and chowders because it allows steady simmering with little risk of scorching. Heavy stainless steel and aluminum pots are also good choices. A very big one—at least 10-quart capacity—will enable you to double most recipes. Refrigerate or freeze what's left for a later meal.

Hearty Pork Stew

For a quick supper, serve steaming bowls of stew with corn sticks. Double the recipe, and freeze half of it for later use. Thaw the stew, reheat, and serve.

1 pound lean boneless pork loin
Vegetable cooking spray
1 cup chopped onion
¼ teaspoon garlic powder
¼ teaspoon onion powder
1 (14½-ounce) can no-salt-added whole peeled tomatoes, undrained
2 cups low-sodium chicken broth, undiluted
1 (10-ounce) package frozen baby lima beans
1 (10-ounce) package frozen whole kernel corn
1 (4-ounce) can chopped green chiles, undrained
½ teaspoon salt
½ teaspoon hot sauce
¼ teaspoon freshly ground pepper
2 tablespoons all-purpose flour
2 tablespoons water

Trim fat from pork; cut pork into ½-inch cubes. Coat a Dutch oven with cooking spray, and place over medium-high heat until hot. Add pork and onion; sprinkle with garlic powder and onion powder. Cook 5 minutes or until pork is browned and onion is tender, stirring frequently. Drain pork mixture; wipe pan with a paper towel.

Return pork mixture to Dutch oven; add tomatoes, crushing tomatoes with the back of a wooden spoon. Add broth and next 6 ingredients. Bring to a boil over high heat. Cover, reduce heat, and simmer 40 to 50 minutes or until pork and vegetables are tender.

Combine flour and water in a small bowl, stirring until smooth. Add flour mixture to soup. Cook soup, stirring constantly, an additional 5 minutes or until mixture thickens. Yield: 6 servings.

PER SERVING: 276 CALORIES (27% FROM FAT)
FAT 8.3G (SATURATED FAT 2.7G)
PROTEIN 21.2G   CARBOHYDRATE 29.5G
CHOLESTEROL 50MG   SODIUM 416MG

Hearty Pork Stew

ORIENTAL PORK STEW

Nut-flavored basmati rice can be found in Indian and Middle Eastern food markets as well as in the larger supermarkets.

1½ cups water
¼ cup low-sodium soy sauce
2 tablespoons plus 2 teaspoons blackstrap molasses
3 cloves garlic
3 thin slices peeled gingerroot
Vegetable cooking spray
1½ pounds lean, boneless pork loin, cut into 1-inch cubes
⅛ teaspoon anise seeds
⅛ teaspoon crushed red pepper
1½ cups chopped fennel bulb
1 cup julienne-sliced sweet red pepper
4 green onions, diagonally sliced into 1-inch pieces
2 tablespoons dry sherry
1 tablespoon cornstarch
6 cups cooked white basmati or long-grain rice (cooked without salt or fat)

Combine first 5 ingredients in container of an electric blender. Cover and process 30 seconds or until smooth; set aside.

Coat a large Dutch oven with cooking spray; place over high heat until hot. Add pork, and cook 4 minutes, browning well on all sides. Add soy sauce mixture, anise seeds, and crushed red pepper; bring to a boil. Cover, reduce heat, and simmer 30 minutes or until pork is tender.

Add fennel, sweet red pepper, and green onions to pork mixture; stir well. Cover and simmer 4 minutes or until vegetables are crisp-tender.

Combine sherry and cornstarch; stir well. Add to pan. Bring to a boil, and cook 1 minute, stirring constantly. Serve over rice. Yield: 6 servings.

PER SERVING: 454 CALORIES (18% FROM FAT)
FAT 9.1G (SATURATED FAT 3.0G)
PROTEIN 29.1G CARBOHYDRATE 61.6G
CHOLESTEROL 68MG SODIUM 403MG

SOUTHWESTERN PORK STEW

1 pound lean, boneless pork loin
1½ teaspoons ground cumin
¼ teaspoon salt
¼ teaspoon ground cinnamon
⅛ teaspoon ground red pepper
2 teaspoons vegetable oil
1¾ cups coarsely chopped onion
1 cup (¾-inch) pieces green pepper
2 cloves garlic, minced
3 cups peeled, cubed baking potato (about 1 pound)
1 cup no-salt-added vegetable juice cocktail
½ cup water
1 (14½-ounce) can Mexican-style stewed tomatoes with jalapeño peppers and spices, undrained
1 (10-ounce) package frozen whole kernel corn, thawed and drained
Chopped fresh cilantro (optional)

Trim fat from pork. Cut pork into ¾-inch cubes. Combine next 4 ingredients in a large heavy-duty, zip-top plastic bag. Add pork; seal bag, shaking to coat pork with spices.

Heat oil in a Dutch oven over medium heat. Add pork; cook 5 minutes. Add onion, green pepper, and garlic; sauté 3 minutes. Stir in potato and next 3 ingredients; bring to a boil. Cover, reduce heat, and simmer 25 minutes. Stir in corn. Cover and simmer 35 minutes. Ladle stew into bowls; garnish with cilantro, if desired. Yield: 6 (1½-cup) servings.

PER SERVING: 287 CALORIES (24% FROM FAT)
FAT 7.8G (SATURATED FAT 2.3G)
PROTEIN 20.7G CARBOHYDRATE 35.6G
CHOLESTEROL 45MG SODIUM 340MG

BRUNSWICK STEW

3 (4-ounce) skinned, boned chicken breast
   halves
2 cups water
3 tablespoons chopped fresh parsley
½ teaspoon salt
½ teaspoon dried thyme
1 bay leaf
1½ cups diced potato
1 cup sliced celery
1 medium onion, sliced
1 (14½-ounce) can no-salt-added whole
   tomatoes, undrained and chopped
1 (10-ounce) package frozen baby lima beans,
   thawed
1 (10-ounce) package frozen whole kernel
   corn, thawed
2 teaspoons low-sodium Worcestershire sauce
½ teaspoon black pepper
¼ teaspoon garlic powder
¼ teaspoon ground red pepper

Trim fat from chicken. Place chicken, 2 cups
water, chopped parsley, salt, thyme, and bay leaf in
a large Dutch oven. Bring chicken mixture to a
boil; cover, reduce heat, and simmer 20 minutes or
until chicken is done.

Remove chicken from broth; shred chicken, and
place in a medium bowl. Set aside. Remove and
discard bay leaf.

Skim and discard fat from broth; return chicken
to pan. Add potato, celery, onion, tomato, lima
beans, and corn, stirring well to combine.

Add Worcestershire sauce and remaining ingredients; stir well. Bring mixture to a boil; cover,
reduce heat, and simmer 2 hours, stirring frequently. Yield: 6 (1⅓-cup) servings.

PER SERVING: 237 CALORIES (8% FROM FAT)
FAT 2.1G (SATURATED FAT 0.5G)
PROTEIN 19.9G   CARBOHYDRATE 35.5G
CHOLESTEROL 35MG   SODIUM 334MG

TURKEY-VEGETABLE STEW

½ cup all-purpose flour, divided
1½ pounds turkey tenderloin, cut into 1-inch
   pieces
Vegetable cooking spray
1 tablespoon vegetable oil
½ cup chopped onion
2 cups cubed peeled kohlrabi (about 1 pound)
1½ cups coarsely chopped cabbage
1 cup sliced carrot
6 small red potatoes, peeled and quartered
   (about ¾ pound)
½ to 1 teaspoon dried thyme
½ teaspoon dried sage
2 (13¾-ounce) cans no-salt-added chicken
   broth
2 cups small fresh broccoli flowerets
2 (14½-ounce) cans no-salt-added whole
   tomatoes, drained and coarsely chopped
½ cup water
1 teaspoon salt
¼ teaspoon pepper

Place ¼ cup flour in a large heavy-duty, zip-top
plastic bag. Add turkey; seal bag, and shake to coat.

Coat a Dutch oven with cooking spray; add vegetable oil, and place over medium-high heat until
hot. Add turkey and onion; cook 6 minutes or until
turkey loses its pink color. Add kohlrabi and next 6
ingredients; bring to a boil. Cover, reduce heat, and
simmer 20 minutes or until potato is tender. Add
broccoli and tomato; cook, uncovered, 5 minutes or
until broccoli is tender.

Place remaining ¼ cup flour in a bowl. Gradually
add ½ cup water, stirring with a wire whisk until
blended; add to stew. Stir in salt and pepper. Cook
over medium heat 5 minutes or until thickened,
stirring frequently. Yield: 6 (1½-cup) servings.

PER SERVING: 293 CALORIES (17% FROM FAT)
FAT 5.5G (SATURATED FAT 1.4G)
PROTEIN 30.4G   CARBOHYDRATE 29.1G
CHOLESTEROL 59MG   SODIUM 489MG

White Chili with Tomatillo Salsa

WHITE CHILI WITH TOMATILLO SALSA

Chunks of chicken replace the typical beef in this chili, reducing the calories and fat. Using only white beans creates a hearty chili with a different look.

3 (10½-ounce) cans low-sodium chicken broth, divided
1 (19-ounce) can cannellini beans, drained and divided
1 (16-ounce) can navy beans, drained and divided
4 cups chopped cooked chicken breast
1 cup chopped onion
1 (16-ounce) package frozen white corn
1 (4-ounce) can chopped green chiles, undrained
1 teaspoon ground cumin
¾ teaspoon dried oregano
¼ teaspoon ground red pepper
Tomatillo Salsa

Place 1 cup broth, ½ cup cannellini beans, and ½ cup navy beans in container of an electric blender or food processor; cover and process until smooth.

Place bean mixture, remaining broth, remaining cannellini beans, remaining navy beans, chicken, and remaining ingredients in a Dutch oven. Bring to a boil; cover, reduce heat, and simmer 30 minutes. Ladle chili into individual bowls. Top servings evenly with Tomatillo Salsa. Yield: 8 (1¼-cup) servings.

TOMATILLO SALSA
½ pound husked, diced tomatillos or diced green tomatoes
¼ cup diced red onion
¼ cup chopped sweet yellow or green pepper
⅛ cup chopped fresh cilantro
1 tablespoon orange juice
½ small jalapeño pepper, seeded and chopped
½ clove garlic, minced
1 teaspoon sugar
Dash of salt

Combine all ingredients in a medium bowl. Cover and chill at least 30 minutes. Yield: 2 cups.

PER SERVING: 311 CALORIES (13% FROM FAT)
FAT 4.4G (SATURATED FAT 1.0G)
PROTEIN 33.5G   CARBOHYDRATE 32.4G
CHOLESTEROL 73MG   SODIUM 365MG

SPICY VEGETABLE CHILI

Vegetable cooking spray
2 teaspoons vegetable oil
1 cup thinly sliced carrot
1 cup chopped onion
½ cup chopped green pepper
3 cloves garlic, minced
2 cups peeled, cubed red potato
1 cup canned no-salt-added beef broth, undiluted
1 cup water
1 cup frozen whole kernel corn, thawed
1 cup commercial chunky salsa
1 (15-ounce) can no-salt-added tomato sauce
1½ tablespoons chili powder
¾ teaspoon ground cumin
¼ teaspoon pepper
1 (15-ounce) can red kidney beans, drained
½ cup (2 ounces) shredded reduced-fat Cheddar cheese
Nonfat sour cream alternative (optional)

Coat a large Dutch oven with cooking spray; add oil, and place over medium-high heat until hot. Add carrot, onion, green pepper, and garlic; sauté until tender. Add potato and next 8 ingredients; bring to a boil. Reduce heat; simmer, uncovered, 30 minutes. Cover and simmer an additional 30 minutes or until potato is tender.

Add beans to pan, and cook, uncovered, 5 minutes. Spoon chili into serving bowls; sprinkle each serving with 1 tablespoon cheese. If desired, top with sour cream. Yield: 6 (1⅓-cup) servings.

PER SERVING: 209 CALORIES (18% FROM FAT)
FAT 4.2G (SATURATED FAT 1.5G)
PROTEIN 10.0G   CARBOHYDRATE 35.2G
CHOLESTEROL 6MG   SODIUM 308MG

Italian Sausage-Black Bean Soup

6 ounces Italian-flavored turkey sausage
¾ cup chopped onion
½ cup chopped carrot
⅓ cup chopped celery
2 cloves garlic, minced
3 (15-ounce) cans black beans, drained and divided
2 (10½-ounce) cans low-sodium chicken broth
1 (14½-ounce) can no-salt-added whole tomatoes, drained and coarsely chopped
⅓ cup chopped fresh cilantro
2 tablespoons no-salt-added tomato paste
1 tablespoon fresh lime juice
1 teaspoon ground cumin
¼ teaspoon salt
⅛ teaspoon ground red pepper
¼ cup plus 2 tablespoons nonfat sour cream alternative
Fresh cilantro leaves (optional)

Crumble sausage in a Dutch oven, and add onion, carrot, celery, and garlic. Cook over medium-high heat 5 minutes or until sausage is browned and vegetables are tender, stirring frequently. Add 2 cans black beans, chicken broth, and next 7 ingredients.

Place remaining 1 can black beans in a bowl; mash with a fork, and add to soup mixture. Bring to a boil; reduce heat, and simmer, uncovered, 30 minutes or until thickened. Ladle soup into individual bowls. Top each serving with 1 tablespoon sour cream. Garnish with fresh cilantro leaves, if desired. Yield: 6 (1⅓-cup) servings.

PER SERVING: 290 CALORIES (23% FROM FAT)
FAT 7.4G (SATURATED FAT 2.3G)
PROTEIN 18.9G   CARBOHYDRATE 38.9G
CHOLESTEROL 25MG   SODIUM 719MG

Shrimp-Chicken Gumbo

4 (6-ounce) skinned chicken breast halves
2 quarts water
½ cup all-purpose flour
Vegetable cooking spray
1 tablespoon vegetable oil
2 cups chopped onion
1¾ cups chopped celery
1½ cups chopped green pepper
½ cup chopped green onions
4 cloves garlic, minced
1½ teaspoons dried thyme
1 teaspoon dried oregano
½ teaspoon pepper
3 bay leaves
1 (13¾-ounce) can no-salt-added chicken broth
1 (6-ounce) can no-salt-added tomato paste
½ pound low-fat smoked turkey sausage, sliced
1 pound unpeeled medium-size fresh shrimp
6 cups cooked long-grain rice (cooked without salt or fat)

Combine chicken and water in a Dutch oven; bring to a boil. Reduce heat; simmer 45 minutes. Cover; chill 8 hours. Remove chicken; skim and discard fat from broth, reserving broth. Bone and chop chicken.

Place flour in a 15- x 10- x 1-inch jellyroll pan. Bake at 350° for 1 hour or until very brown, stirring every 15 minutes. Set aside.

Coat a Dutch oven with cooking spray; add oil. Place over medium heat until hot. Add onion and next 4 ingredients; sauté until tender. Add thyme and next 3 ingredients. Add browned flour; stir until smooth. Add reserved broth, chicken, canned broth, tomato paste, and sausage. Bring to a boil; reduce heat, and simmer, uncovered, 1 hour.

Peel and devein shrimp; add to broth mixture. Cover and simmer 10 minutes or until shrimp turn pink. Discard bay leaves. Serve over rice. Yield: 12 (1½-cup) servings.

PER SERVING: 264 CALORIES (12% FROM FAT)
FAT 3.6G (SATURATED FAT 2.5G)
PROTEIN 20.2G   CARBOHYDRATE 36.1G
CHOLESTEROL 75MG   SODIUM 279MG

Shrimp-Chicken Gumbo

SHRIMP AND CORN CHOWDER

1 poblano pepper, roasted and peeled
1 sweet red pepper, roasted and peeled
Vegetable cooking spray
½ cup chopped onion
2 cloves garlic, minced
2 (10-ounce) packages frozen whole kernel
   corn, thawed
2 cups 1% low-fat milk, divided
⅔ cup evaporated skimmed milk
1½ teaspoons cornstarch
3 tablespoons water
¼ teaspoon salt
1 pound unpeeled medium-size fresh shrimp
2 tablespoons minced fresh cilantro

Dice peppers; set aside.

Coat a nonstick skillet with cooking spray; place over medium-high heat until hot. Add onion and garlic; sauté until tender.

Position knife blade in food processor bowl; add onion mixture and corn. Process until smooth. Transfer mixture to a saucepan; stir in 1 cup milk. Cook over medium heat, stirring constantly, 15 minutes. Stir in remaining 1 cup milk. Cover; cook over medium-low heat 10 minutes, stirring occasionally.

Pour corn mixture into a wire-mesh strainer; press to squeeze out liquid. Discard remaining pulp. Return corn mixture to saucepan, and stir in evaporated milk.

Combine cornstarch and water; stir into corn mixture. Add diced pepper and salt; stir well. Bring to a boil; reduce heat, and simmer, uncovered, 20 minutes or until thickened, stirring frequently.

Peel and devein shrimp. Add shrimp to corn mixture; cook over medium heat 3 to 5 minutes or until shrimp turn pink. Stir in minced cilantro. Ladle chowder into individual serving bowls. Yield: 4 (1½-cup) servings.

Note: Instructions for roasting and peeling peppers may be found on page 125.

PER SERVING: 333 CALORIES (12% FROM FAT)
FAT 4.4G (SATURATED FAT 1.4G)
PROTEIN 29.9G   CARBOHYDRATE 47.9G
CHOLESTEROL 136MG   SODIUM 391MG

SAFFRON-SHRIMP SOUP

Olive oil-flavored vegetable cooking spray
1 cup chopped onion
1 cup chopped green pepper
1 cup chopped sweet red pepper
2 cloves garlic, minced
3 cups water
1 cup no-salt-added tomato juice
½ cup Chablis or other dry white wine
1⅔ cups peeled, seeded, and chopped tomato
¼ cup minced fresh parsley
1 teaspoon chicken-flavored bouillon granules
¼ teaspoon crushed saffron
¼ teaspoon crushed red pepper
¾ pound medium-size fresh shrimp, peeled
   and deveined
Sourdough Croutons

Coat a large Dutch oven with cooking spray; place over medium-high heat until hot. Add onion and next 3 ingredients; sauté until tender.

Add water and next 7 ingredients; bring to a boil. Cover, reduce heat, and simmer 30 minutes. Add shrimp, stirring well. Simmer, uncovered, an additional 10 minutes or until shrimp are done. Ladle soup into individual bowls. Top each with Sourdough Croutons. Yield: 4 (1½-cup) servings.

SOURDOUGH CROUTONS

3 (1-ounce) slices sourdough bread (½ inch
   thick)
2 teaspoons olive oil
¼ teaspoon garlic powder

Cut bread into ½-inch cubes. Combine olive oil and garlic powder in a small bowl, stirring well. Add bread cubes, and toss gently to coat well. Arrange bread cubes in a single layer in a 15- x 10- x 1-inch jellyroll pan. Bake at 275° for 30 to 35 minutes or until golden, stirring after 15 minutes. Remove croutons from oven, and cool completely. Yield: 1⅔ cups.

PER SERVING: 206 CALORIES (20% FROM FAT)
FAT 4.6G (SATURATED FAT 0.6G)
PROTEIN 17.6G   CARBOHYDRATE 25.3G
CHOLESTEROL 97MG   SODIUM 423MG

Saffron-Shrimp Soup

STIR-FRY & STOVETOP

*T*he Chinese introduced Americans to that one-dish wonder, stir-fry, and its popularity has never waned. Nowadays even small towns in the United States boast a Chinese restaurant.

The pages that follow feature several Oriental-flavored stir-fries and an assortment of popular stovetop meals, including Beef Stroganoff (page 84), two kinds of ragout, and Spicy Red Beans and Chunky Rice (page 98). And if you've never tried a seafood boil, go for it! Easy-to-follow instructions are on page 93.

Teriyaki Beef and Sweet Peppers (Recipe follows on page 78)

CURRIED STEAK WITH BABY VEGETABLES

(pictured on page 2)

1 (1-pound) lean flank steak
¼ cup dry sherry
2 tablespoons reduced-sodium soy sauce
1 teaspoon peeled, grated gingerroot
½ teaspoon curry powder
¼ teaspoon ground coriander
¼ teaspoon dry mustard
Vegetable cooking spray
1 teaspoon vegetable oil
2 cloves garlic, minced
1 small onion, sliced
1 (8-ounce) package frozen baby corn, thawed
9 baby zucchini, halved lengthwise
3 cups cooked long-grain rice (cooked without salt or fat)
¼ cup finely chopped sweet red pepper

Partially freeze steak; trim fat from steak. Slice steak diagonally across grain into ¼-inch strips.

Combine sherry and next 5 ingredients in a small bowl; stir well, and set aside.

Coat a wok or large nonstick skillet with cooking spray; add oil. Heat at medium-high (375°) until hot. Add steak strips and garlic; stir-fry 5 minutes. Remove steak strips from wok, and set aside. Add onion, corn, and zucchini to wok; stir-fry 1 minute. Add steak strips and reserved sherry mixture; cook, stirring constantly, 4 minutes. Serve over cooked rice, and sprinkle with chopped sweet red pepper. Yield: 6 servings.

PER SERVING: 298 CALORIES (26% FROM FAT)
FAT 8.7G (SATURATED FAT 3.3G)
PROTEIN 19.2G   CARBOHYDRATE 35.7G
CHOLESTEROL 38MG   SODIUM 221MG

TERIYAKI BEEF AND SWEET PEPPERS

(pictured on page 76)

¾ pound lean boneless top round steak
¼ cup low-sodium soy sauce
2 tablespoons unsweetened pineapple juice
2 teaspoons cornstarch
1 teaspoon instant minced garlic
Vegetable cooking spray
2 teaspoons vegetable oil
1 medium-size sweet red pepper, seeded and cut into very thin strips
1 medium-size sweet yellow pepper, seeded and cut into very thin strips
1 medium-size green pepper, seeded and cut into very thin strips
2 cups cooked long-grain rice (cooked without salt or fat)

Partially freeze steak; trim fat from steak. Slice steak diagonally across grain into ¼-inch strips.

Combine soy sauce and next 3 ingredients in a small bowl; stir well, and set aside.

Coat a wok or nonstick skillet with cooking spray; drizzle oil around top of wok, coating sides. Heat at medium-high (375°) until hot. Add steak; stir-fry 2 minutes. Add peppers; stir-fry 4 minutes or until steak is browned. Add reserved cornstarch mixture to steak mixture. Cook, stirring constantly, until thickened. Serve over rice. Yield: 4 servings.

PER SERVING: 286 CALORIES (23% FROM FAT)
FAT 7.3G (SATURATED FAT 2.1G)
PROTEIN 21.7G   CARBOHYDRATE 30.4G
CHOLESTEROL 49MG   SODIUM 441MG

FYI

The wok is excellent for cooking with little or no fat. To cook vegetables and meat, cut into small pieces; then toss during cooking to prevent sticking and promote even cooking.

Stir-Fried Beef and Vegetables

STIR-FRIED BEEF AND VEGETABLES

1½ pounds lean boneless top round steak
½ cup water
3 tablespoons low-sodium soy sauce
3 cloves garlic, minced
½ teaspoon pepper
Vegetable cooking spray
4½ cups fresh broccoli flowerets
3 cups sliced fresh mushrooms
1 small sweet red pepper, cut into very thin strips
18 pearl onions, peeled
1 (10-ounce) package frozen French-style green beans, thawed
2 teaspoons cornstarch
¼ cup water
8 cups cooked rice (cooked without salt or fat)

Partially freeze steak; trim fat from steak. Slice steak diagonally across grain into ¼-inch strips. Place steak in a heavy-duty, zip-top plastic bag.

Combine ½ cup water and next 3 ingredients; stir well. Pour over steak; seal bag, and shake until steak is well coated. Marinate in refrigerator 2 to 4 hours, turning bag occasionally.

Remove steak from marinade, reserving marinade. Coat a wok or large nonstick skillet with cooking spray. Heat at medium-high heat (375°) until hot. Add steak, and stir-fry 3 minutes. Add broccoli and next 3 ingredients; stir-fry 5 minutes or until vegetables are crisp-tender. Add green beans, and stir-fry 1 minute.

Combine cornstarch, marinade, and ¼ cup water, stirring well; add to steak mixture. Cook, stirring constantly, until mixture is thickened. Serve over rice. Yield: 8 servings.

PER SERVING: 379 CALORIES (10% FROM FAT)
FAT 4.1G (SATURATED FAT 1.3G)
PROTEIN 26.3G   CARBOHYDRATE 57.8G
CHOLESTEROL 48MG   SODIUM 208MG

TANGY BEEF WITH GINGER

1 pound lean boneless beef sirloin steak
2 teaspoons peeled, minced gingerroot
½ teaspoon grated tangerine or orange rind
½ cup fresh tangerine or orange juice
2 tablespoons dry sherry
2 tablespoons low-sodium soy sauce
2 teaspoons cornstarch
½ pound fresh snow pea pods
Vegetable cooking spray
1 teaspoon dark sesame oil
1 cup fresh bean sprouts
¾ cup diagonally sliced celery
3 cups cooked long-grain rice (cooked without
    salt or fat)

Partially freeze steak; trim fat from steak. Slice steak diagonally across grain into ¼-inch strips; place strips in a bowl.

Combine gingerroot and next 4 ingredients; stir well. Pour over steak strips; toss to coat. Cover and marinate in refrigerator at least 30 minutes.

Drain steak strips, reserving marinade. Combine reserved marinade and cornstarch; stir well, and set aside. Wash snow peas; trim ends, remove strings, and set aside.

Coat a wok or large nonstick skillet with cooking spray; add oil. Heat at medium-high (375°) until hot. Add steak strips, and stir-fry 5 minutes. Remove from wok.

Add snow peas, bean sprouts, and celery to wok; stir-fry 3 minutes. Add steak strips and marinade mixture; stir-fry 2 to 3 minutes or until mixture is slightly thickened. Serve steak mixture over rice. Yield: 6 servings.

PER SERVING: 253 CALORIES (17% FROM FAT)
FAT 4.9G (SATURATED FAT 1.5G)
PROTEIN 19.3G   CARBOHYDRATE 31.0G
CHOLESTEROL 45MG   SODIUM 189MG

LEMON-HONEY PORK

Serve this tasty stir-fry over cooked rice or angel hair pasta if you don't have rice noodles.

¾ pound lean boneless pork loin
2 tablespoons lemon juice
1 tablespoon honey
1 tablespoon low-sodium soy sauce
1 tablespoon cornstarch
½ cup water
Vegetable cooking spray
1 teaspoon vegetable oil
1 large carrot, scraped and diagonally sliced
1 (6-ounce) package frozen snow pea pods,
    thawed
¼ cup sliced green onions
1 cup fresh bean sprouts, washed and drained
2 cups cooked rice noodles (cooked without
    salt or fat)

Partially freeze pork; trim fat from pork. Slice pork diagonally across grain into 2- x ½-inch strips; set aside.

Combine lemon juice, honey, and soy sauce. Combine cornstarch and water, stirring well. Add to honey mixture; set aside.

Coat a wok or a large nonstick skillet with cooking spray; add oil. Heat at medium-high (375°) until hot. Add pork; stir-fry 3 minutes or until browned. Remove from wok; pat dry with paper towels. Set aside.

Add carrot; stir-fry 3 or 4 minutes or until crisp-tender. Add snow peas, green onions, and bean sprouts; stir-fry 1 minute. Return pork to wok.

Pour reserved lemon juice mixture over pork mixture in wok. Cook, stirring constantly, until mixture is thickened. For each serving, spoon 1 cup pork mixture over ½ cup cooked rice noodles. Yield: 4 servings.

PER SERVING: 350 CALORIES (23% FROM FAT)
FAT 8.8G (SATURATED FAT 2.5G)
PROTEIN 24.3G   CARBOHYDRATE 43.1G
CHOLESTEROL 54MG   SODIUM 189MG

PORK AND VEGETABLE STIR-FRY

1 pound lean boneless pork loin
½ teaspoon dried tarragon
½ teaspoon lemon-pepper seasoning
¼ teaspoon salt
⅛ teaspoon garlic powder
1½ teaspoons cornstarch
¼ cup water
¼ cup Chablis or other dry white wine
3 tablespoons lemon juice
1 teaspoon sugar
Vegetable cooking spray
1½ cups sliced carrot
1¼ cups cubed turnips
1 leek, cut into ½-inch pieces
1¼ cups sliced celery
3 cups cooked long-grain rice (cooked without salt or fat)

Partially freeze pork; trim fat, and slice pork diagonally across grain into 2- x ¼-inch strips.

Combine tarragon, lemon-pepper seasoning, salt, and garlic powder; sprinkle mixture evenly over pork strips, tossing to coat. Set pork strips aside.

Combine cornstarch, water, wine, lemon juice, and sugar in a bowl; stir well. Set mixture aside.

Coat a wok or large nonstick skillet with cooking spray; heat at medium-high (375°) until hot. Add pork; stir-fry 5 to 7 minutes or until browned. Remove pork from wok. Drain and pat dry with paper towels; set aside. Wipe drippings from wok with a paper towel.

Coat wok with cooking spray. Add sliced carrot and turnips; stir-fry 5 to 7 minutes or until vegetables are crisp-tender. Add leek and celery; stir-fry 3 minutes. Add pork and reserved cornstarch mixture to wok; bring mixture to a boil. Cook, stirring constantly, until thickened. Serve over cooked rice. Yield: 6 servings.

PER SERVING: 258 CALORIES (11% FROM FAT)
FAT 3.2G (SATURATED FAT 1.0G)
PROTEIN 19.6G   CARBOHYDRATE 36.9G
CHOLESTEROL 53MG   SODIUM 225MG

TURKEY STIR-FRY

1 cup canned no-salt-added chicken broth, undiluted
¼ cup reduced-sodium soy sauce
2 tablespoons cornstarch
1 tablespoon peeled, grated gingerroot
⅛ teaspoon crushed red pepper
⅛ teaspoon crushed Szechuan peppercorns
1 clove garlic, minced
1 tablespoon dark sesame oil
1 pound turkey breast slices, cut into thin strips
4 cups sliced bok choy
1 cup sliced fresh mushrooms
½ pound fresh asparagus, trimmed and diagonally sliced into 1-inch pieces
5 green onions, diagonally sliced into 1-inch pieces
1 (8-ounce) can sliced water chestnuts, drained
3 cups cooked long-grain rice (cooked without salt or fat)

Combine first 7 ingredients in a small bowl; stir well, and set aside.

Heat a wok or large nonstick skillet at medium-high (375°) until hot; add oil. Add turkey to wok; stir-fry 3 minutes. Remove from wok; set aside. Add bok choy and next 3 ingredients; stir-fry 2 minutes. Add broth mixture and water chestnuts; stir well.

Return turkey to wok; cook, stirring constantly, until sauce is thickened. For each serving, spoon 1 cup turkey mixture over ½ cup cooked rice. Yield: 6 servings.

PER SERVING: 276 CALORIES (13% FROM FAT)
FAT 4.1G (SATURATED FAT 0.7G)
PROTEIN 22.9G   CARBOHYDRATE 36.2G
CHOLESTEROL 45MG   SODIUM 429MG

Sweet-and-Sour Scallops

SWEET-AND-SOUR SCALLOPS

The sweet flavor of the scallops is enhanced by the sweetness of the pineapple and grapes in this flavorful stir-fry.

1 (8-ounce) can pineapple chunks in juice, undrained
2 tablespoons cornstarch
2 tablespoons brown sugar
2 tablespoons cider vinegar
2 tablespoons low-sodium soy sauce
½ teaspoon chicken-flavored bouillon granules
⅛ teaspoon ground ginger
Vegetable cooking spray
1 teaspoon safflower oil
1 medium-size green pepper, cut into ¾-inch pieces
1 pound fresh sea scallops
½ cup seedless red grapes, halved
2 cups cooked long-grain rice (cooked without salt or fat)

Drain pineapple chunks, reserving juice. Set pineapple aside. Add water to juice to make ½ cup liquid.

Combine cornstarch and next 5 ingredients in a small bowl; stir well. Add pineapple juice mixture; stir well. Set aside.

Coat a wok or large nonstick skillet with cooking spray; add oil. Heat at medium-high (375°) until hot. Add green pepper; stir-fry 1 minute. Add scallops and cornstarch mixture; cook, stirring constantly, 3 to 4 minutes or until scallops are opaque and mixture is slightly thickened. Stir in grapes and reserved pineapple chunks.

To serve, spoon ½ cup rice onto each of 4 individual serving plates; spoon scallop mixture evenly over rice. Yield: 4 servings.

PER SERVING: 335 CALORIES (8% FROM FAT)
FAT 2.8G (SATURATED FAT 0.3G)
PROTEIN 22.2G   CARBOHYDRATE 53.1G
CHOLESTEROL 37MG   SODIUM 485MG

STIR-FRY OF SCALLOPS

1 tablespoon cornstarch, divided
1 tablespoon water
¾ pound bay scallops
Vegetable cooking spray
2 teaspoons peanut oil, divided
1 tablespoon minced garlic, divided
¼ cup canned low-sodium chicken broth, undiluted
1 tablespoon dry vermouth
½ teaspoon sugar
4 ounces fresh snow pea pods
¾ cup sliced leek
½ cup thinly sliced sweet red pepper
2 cups sliced fresh mushrooms
4 cups cooked long-grain rice (cooked without salt or fat)

Combine 1½ teaspoons cornstarch and water in a small bowl; stir well. Add scallops, tossing gently. Set aside.

Coat a wok or large nonstick skillet with cooking spray; add 1 teaspoon oil. Heat at medium high (375°) until hot. Add 1½ teaspoons garlic; sauté 10 seconds. Add scallop mixture, and sauté 2 minutes. Remove scallop mixture from wok; set aside. Wipe drippings from wok with a paper towel.

Combine chicken broth, vermouth, remaining 1½ teaspoons cornstarch, and sugar in a small bowl; stir well. Set aside.

Wash snow peas; trim ends, and remove strings. Place remaining 1 teaspoon oil in wok; heat at medium-high until hot. Add remaining 1½ teaspoons garlic, snow peas, leek, and sweet red pepper; sauté 2 minutes. Add mushrooms; sauté 2 minutes. Add scallop mixture and chicken broth mixture; cook, stirring constantly, until mixture is thickened and thoroughly heated. Serve over rice. Yield: 4 servings.

PER SERVING: 391 CALORIES (9% FROM FAT)
FAT 3.8G (SATURATED FAT 0.7G)
PROTEIN 18.6G   CARBOHYDRATE 68.6G
CHOLESTEROL 22MG   SODIUM 118MG

BEEF STROGANOFF

This recipe calls for noodles made without egg yolks to keep down the cholesterol content. You may use regular noodles or rice if you prefer.

1 (1-pound) lean boneless beef sirloin steak
Vegetable cooking spray
2 cups sliced fresh mushrooms
1 cup chopped onion
1½ tablespoons reduced-calorie margarine
1½ tablespoons all-purpose flour
1 cup water
1 teaspoon beef-flavored bouillon granules
½ cup plain nonfat yogurt
¼ cup low-fat sour cream
¼ cup Burgundy or other dry red wine
¼ teaspoon salt
¾ teaspoon pepper
3 cups cooked medium noodles made without
    egg yolks (cooked without salt or fat)

Partially freeze steak; trim fat from steak. Slice steak into thin strips. Coat a Dutch oven with cooking spray; place over medium-high heat until hot. Add steak, mushrooms, and onion; sauté 10 minutes or until steak is browned and vegetables are tender. Remove from heat; drain and pat dry with paper towels.

Melt margarine in a heavy saucepan over low heat; add flour, stirring until smooth. Cook 1 minute, stirring constantly. Gradually add water and bouillon granules; cook over medium heat, stirring constantly, until thickened and bubbly.

Combine yogurt (at room temperature) and next 4 ingredients, stirring well; add yogurt mixture and steak mixture to skillet. Cook over low heat 5 minutes or until thoroughly heated, stirring frequently. (Do not boil.) Serve steak mixture over cooked noodles. Yield: 6 servings.

PER SERVING: 297 CALORIES (28% FROM FAT)
FAT 9.1G (SATURATED FAT 2.7G)
PROTEIN 26.2G   CARBOHYDRATE 26.8G
CHOLESTEROL 62MG   SODIUM 376MG

BEEF RAGOUT WITH WINTER SQUASH

2 pounds lean, boneless beef round steak
Vegetable cooking spray
2 cups coarsely chopped onion
2 cloves garlic, minced
3 cups sliced fresh mushrooms
2½ cups diagonally sliced carrot
2 (14½-ounce) cans Italian-style tomatoes,
    undrained
1 cup water
2 teaspoons dried thyme
½ teaspoon pepper
4 cups peeled, cubed butternut squash
8 cups cooked medium egg noodles (cooked
    without salt or fat)
Fresh parsley sprigs (optional)

Trim fat from steak. Cut steak into 1-inch cubes. Coat a Dutch oven with cooking spray; place over medium heat until hot. Add steak; cook 5 minutes or until steak loses its pink color. Remove from pan. Drain; set aside.

Wipe drippings from pan with a paper towel; recoat pan with cooking spray, and place over medium heat until hot. Add onion and garlic; sauté 3 minutes, stirring frequently. Return steak to pan. Add mushrooms and next 5 ingredients; bring to a boil. Cover, reduce heat, and simmer 1 hour. Add squash; cover and simmer 30 minutes or until steak is tender. For each serving, spoon 1½ cups steak mixture over 1 cup noodles. Garnish with parsley, if desired. Yield: 8 servings.

Note: Ragout freezes well. Spoon ragout into an airtight container; store in freezer up to 1 week or in refrigerator up to 3 days. To serve, thaw in refrigerator. Place in a large saucepan over medium heat, and cook 10 minutes or until thoroughly heated, stirring occasionally.

PER SERVING: 469 CALORIES (16% FROM FAT)
FAT 8.2G (SATURATED FAT 2.4G)
PROTEIN 37.8G   CARBOHYDRATE 61.3G
CHOLESTEROL 124MG   SODIUM 214MG

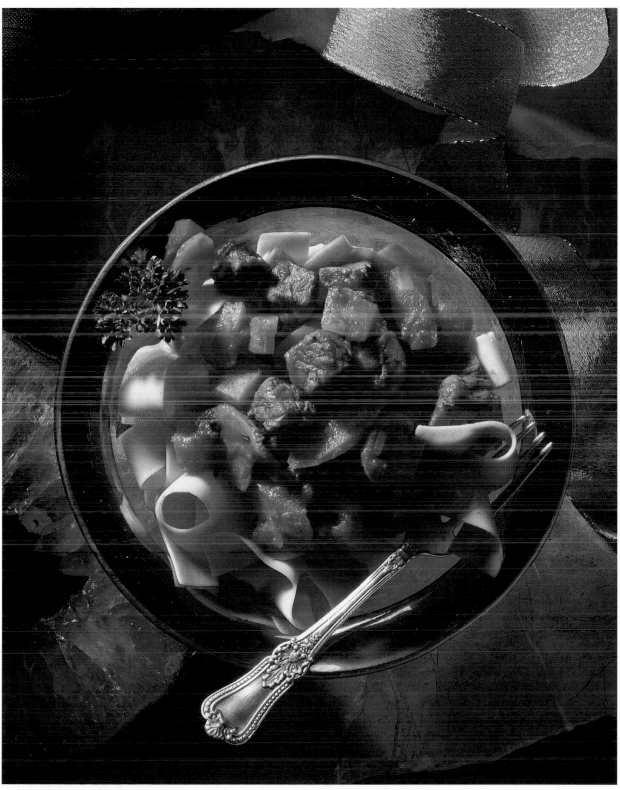

Beef Ragout with Winter Squash

Braised Veal Shanks with Vegetables

BRAISED VEAL SHANKS WITH VEGETABLES

6 (5-ounce) veal shanks
Vegetable cooking spray
½ cup Chablis or other dry white wine
½ cup chopped onion
½ cup thinly sliced celery
½ cup diced zucchini
½ cup shredded carrot
1 clove garlic, sliced
2 cups canned no-salt-added chicken broth, undiluted
2 tablespoons no-salt-added tomato paste
¼ teaspoon salt
¼ teaspoon pepper
12 small round red potatoes (about 1½ pounds)
1 medium carrot, cut into very thin strips
1 small zucchini, cut into very thin strips

Trim fat from veal. Coat a Dutch oven with cooking spray; place over medium-high heat until hot. Add veal; cook 3 minutes on each side or until browned. Drain and pat dry with paper towels. Wipe drippings from pan with a paper towel.

Coat pan with cooking spray. Add wine and next 5 ingredients; bring to a boil, and cook 4 minutes over medium-high heat. Return veal to pan. Stir in broth, tomato paste, salt, and pepper. Bring to a boil; cover, reduce heat, and simmer 1 hour or until veal is tender. Transfer veal to a platter; keep warm. Reserve vegetable-broth mixture.

Cook potatoes in boiling water to cover 15 minutes or until tender; drain and cool slightly. Cut potatoes in quarters; set aside.

Arrange carrot and zucchini strips in a vegetable steamer over boiling water. Cover and steam 3 to 4 minutes or until crisp-tender.

Position knife blade in food processor bowl; add reserved vegetable-broth mixture, and process until smooth. Divide pureed vegetable mixture among 6 serving plates; top with veal. Arrange potato, carrot, and zucchini around veal. Yield: 6 servings.

PER SERVING: 257 CALORIES (28% FROM FAT)
FAT 8.0G (SATURATED FAT 3.1G)
PROTEIN 24.5G   CARBOHYDRATE 21.0G
CHOLESTEROL 93MG   SODIUM 251MG

TUSCAN-STYLE VEAL AND PASTA

2 cups peeled, cubed eggplant (about 1 pound)
2 cups cubed yellow squash (about 1 pound)
½ pound small fresh mushrooms
2 tablespoons balsamic vinegar, divided
2 teaspoons olive oil
1 pound lean ground veal
1 cup chopped onion
¾ teaspoon salt, divided
2 cloves garlic, minced
½ teaspoon crushed red pepper
2 (14½-ounce) cans no-salt-added whole tomatoes, undrained and coarsely chopped
6 cups cooked mostaccioli (tubular pasta), cooked without salt or fat
¼ cup freshly grated Parmesan cheese
¼ cup minced fresh basil

Arrange eggplant, squash, and mushrooms in a single layer in a 15- x 10- x 1-inch jellyroll pan; drizzle 1 tablespoon vinegar and oil over vegetables. Bake at 400° for 8 minutes. Turn vegetables over, and bake an additional 10 minutes or until tender and browned. Set aside.

Combine veal, onion, ¼ teaspoon salt, and garlic in a large nonstick skillet. Cook over medium heat until veal is browned, stirring until veal crumbles. Drain and pat dry with paper towels; wipe drippings from pan with a paper towel. Return veal to skillet. Add remaining ½ teaspoon salt, red pepper, and tomato to skillet; stir well. Bring to a boil; reduce heat, and simmer, uncovered, 10 minutes, stirring occasionally.

Combine vegetable mixture, veal mixture, pasta, and remaining 1 tablespoon vinegar in a large bowl; toss well. Sprinkle with cheese and basil. Yield: 6 (2-cup) servings.

PER SERVING: 397 CALORIES (17% FROM FAT)
FAT 7.7G (SATURATED FAT 2.2G)
PROTEIN 29.3G   CARBOHYDRATE 52.8G
CHOLESTEROL 70MG   SODIUM 443MG

Savory Lamb Ragout

SAVORY LAMB RAGOUT

1½ pounds lean boneless lamb
Vegetable cooking spray
1 large onion, sliced
2 cloves garlic, minced
1 (14½-ounce) can no-salt-added whole
    tomatoes, undrained and chopped
1 cup thinly sliced carrot
⅓ cup Chablis or other dry white wine
1 teaspoon minced fresh rosemary
1 bay leaf
½ teaspoon dried thyme
½ teaspoon chicken-flavored bouillon granules
2 cups cubed yellow squash (about 2 medium)
1 (9-ounce) package frozen artichoke hearts
1 cup sliced fresh mushrooms
4 cups cooked medium egg noodles (cooked
    without salt or fat)
Chopped fresh parsley (optional)
Fresh rosemary sprigs (optional)

Cut lamb into ½-inch cubes. Coat a Dutch oven with cooking spray; place over medium-high heat until hot. Add lamb, onion, and garlic; cook 8 minutes or until lamb is lightly browned on all sides. Drain and pat dry with paper towels. Wipe drippings from pan with a paper towel.

Return lamb mixture to pan. Add tomato and next 6 ingredients. Bring mixture to a boil over medium heat; cover, reduce heat, and simmer 20 minutes or until lamb is tender.

Stir in yellow squash, artichoke hearts, and sliced mushrooms; cook 10 to 12 minutes or until vegetables are tender. Remove and discard bay leaf. Serve lamb ragout over cooked noodles. If desired, garnish with parsley and rosemary sprigs. Yield: 8 servings.

PER SERVING: 293 CALORIES (24% FROM FAT)
FAT 7.8G (SATURATED FAT 2.5G)
PROTEIN 25.3G   CARBOHYDRATE 30.5G
CHOLESTEROL 87MG   SODIUM 140MG

SPICY LAMB WITH COUSCOUS

1 pound lean boneless lamb
Vegetable cooking spray
1½ cups no-salt-added tomato juice
1 cup chopped green pepper
1 cup chopped sweet red pepper
2 tablespoons chopped onion
3 cloves garlic, minced
1 tablespoon lemon juice
½ teaspoon ground coriander
½ teaspoon ground cumin
¼ teaspoon salt
¼ teaspoon ground ginger
¼ teaspoon paprika
1½ cups canned no-salt-added chicken broth,
  undiluted
1 cup couscous, uncooked

Trim fat from lamb; cut lamb into 1-inch pieces. Coat a large saucepan with cooking spray; place over medium-high heat until hot. Add lamb; cook until browned on all sides. Drain and pat dry with paper towels. Wipe drippings from pan with a paper towel.

Return lamb to pan; add tomato juice and next 10 ingredients. Bring mixture to a boil; cover, reduce heat, and simmer 45 minutes or until lamb is tender.

Bring chicken broth to a boil in a medium saucepan. Remove from heat. Add couscous; cover and let stand 5 minutes or until couscous is tender and liquid is absorbed. Fluff couscous with a fork, and transfer to a serving platter; top with lamb mixture. Yield: 4 servings.

PER SERVING: 278 CALORIES (26% FROM FAT)
FAT 8.1G (SATURATED FAT 2.4G)
PROTEIN 28.7G   CARBOHYDRATE 22.4G
CHOLESTEROL 76MG   SODIUM 270MG

QUICK HARVEST PORK SKILLET

Vegetable cooking spray
1 pound lean ground pork
1 cup thinly sliced onion
½ cup thinly sliced celery
¾ cup canned low-sodium chicken broth,
  undiluted
¼ cup Chablis or other dry white wine
1 cup peeled, seeded, and chopped tomato
3 ounces dried fruit bits
½ teaspoon pumpkin pie spice
¼ teaspoon dried thyme
3 cups cooked medium egg noodles (cooked
  without salt or fat)

Coat a large nonstick skillet with cooking spray; place over medium-high heat until hot. Add ground pork, onion, and celery; cook until pork is browned, stirring until it crumbles. Drain and pat pork mixture dry with paper towels. Wipe drippings from skillet with a paper towel.

Return pork mixture to skillet; add chicken broth and next 5 ingredients. Bring to a boil; reduce heat, and simmer 25 minutes or until almost all liquid evaporates and mixture is thoroughly heated, stirring occasionally. Serve pork mixture over noodles. Yield: 6 servings.

PER SERVING: 308 CALORIES (29% FROM FAT)
FAT 9.8G (SATURATED FAT 3.1G)
PROTEIN 19.9G   CARBOHYDRATE 34.4G
CHOLESTEROL 78MG   SODIUM 64MG

Fat Alert

Contrary to what you might think, pork can fit into a low-fat eating plan. Lean pork cuts include the tenderloin, loin chop, and cured or fresh ham. As with other meats, trim away visible fat before cooking.

SKILLET PORK AND NOODLES

1 pound boneless pork center loin, cut into
    thin strips
Vegetable cooking spray
¾ cup chopped onion
2 cloves garlic, minced
1 (14½-ounce) can no-salt-added whole
    tomatoes, undrained and coarsely chopped
½ cup Burgundy or other dry red wine
2 teaspoons dried basil
½ teaspoon dried thyme
¼ teaspoon pepper
2 large carrots, scraped and sliced
2 cups cooked medium egg noodles (cooked
    without salt or fat)
1 tablespoon minced fresh parsley

Cook pork in a large nonstick skillet coated with
cooking spray over medium heat until browned.
Drain and pat dry with paper towels. Wipe drippings from skillet with a paper towel.

Coat skillet with cooking spray. Add chopped
onion and garlic; sauté until tender. Return pork
strips to skillet. Stir in tomato, wine, basil, thyme,
and pepper; bring to a boil. Cover, reduce heat, and
simmer 25 minutes. Stir in carrot; simmer until carrot is tender.

For each serving, spoon 1 cup pork mixture over
½ cup noodles. Sprinkle with minced fresh parsley.
Yield: 4 servings.

PER SERVING: 370 CALORIES (25% FROM FAT)
FAT 10.1G (SATURATED FAT 0.3G)
PROTEIN 31.8G   CARBOHYDRATE 32.8G
CHOLESTEROL 106MG   SODIUM 101MG

SPANISH SAFFRON CHICKEN

6 (4-ounce) skinned, boned chicken breast
    halves
¼ teaspoon freshly ground pepper
Vegetable cooking spray
1 medium onion, sliced
1 clove garlic, minced
½ pound fresh mushrooms, sliced
1 cup water
2 teaspoons paprika
1 teaspoon chicken-flavored bouillon granules
½ teaspoon threads of saffron
1 cup frozen English peas
2 tablespoons sliced pitted ripe olives
¼ cup skim milk
1 tablespoon cornstarch
2 tablespoons water
3 cups cooked long-grain rice (cooked without
    salt or fat)

Sprinkle chicken with pepper. Coat a large
Dutch oven with cooking spray; place over medium
heat until hot. Add chicken, and cook over medium
heat until browned. Remove chicken; drain on
paper towels, and set aside.

Wipe pan drippings from pan with a paper towel.
Coat pan with cooking spray; place over medium-
high heat until hot. Add onion, garlic, and mushrooms; sauté until tender. Add chicken, 1 cup
water, and next 3 ingredients. Bring to a boil.
Cover, reduce heat, and simmer 25 minutes or until
chicken is tender. Remove chicken, and set aside.

Add peas, olives, and milk to Dutch oven. Cover
and simmer 5 minutes. Combine cornstarch and 2
tablespoons water; add to vegetable mixture. Bring
to a boil. Reduce heat; cook, stirring constantly,
until thickened and bubbly. Remove from heat. To
serve, place rice on a serving platter. Arrange chick-
en over rice; top with vegetable mixture. Yield: 6
servings.

PER SERVING: 300 CALORIES (14% FROM FAT)
FAT 4.5G (SATURATED FAT 1.1G)
PROTEIN 30.8G   CARBOHYDRATE 32.7G
CHOLESTEROL 71MG   SODIUM 275MG

CHICKEN AND VEGETABLE COUSCOUS

3 (4-ounce) skinned, boned chicken breast
    halves
2 cups water
½ teaspoon curry powder
Olive oil-flavored vegetable cooking spray
1 teaspoon olive oil
2 cups peeled, cubed eggplant
1½ cups cubed zucchini
1 cup chopped onion
1 cup chopped sweet red pepper
1 clove garlic, minced
1 (14½-ounce) can no-salt-added whole
    tomatoes, undrained and chopped
1 teaspoon chopped fresh mint
½ teaspoon ground cumin
½ teaspoon ground coriander
¼ teaspoon salt
¼ teaspoon pepper
2¼ cups water
1 cup plus 2 tablespoons couscous, uncooked
1 tablespoon pine nuts, toasted

Combine chicken, 2 cups water, and curry powder in a saucepan. Bring to a boil; cover, reduce
heat, and simmer 15 minutes or until chicken is
tender. Remove chicken from broth, and cut into
1-inch pieces; set aside. Skim and discard fat from
broth; reserve broth for another use.

Coat a saucepan with cooking spray; add oil.
Place over medium-high heat until hot. Add eggplant, zucchini, onion, red pepper, and garlic; sauté
until tender. Stir in tomato and next 5 ingredients.
Cover and cook over medium heat 10 minutes. Stir
in chicken; cook until thoroughly heated.

Bring 2¼ cups water to a boil in a medium
saucepan. Remove from heat. Add couscous; cover
and let stand 5 minutes or until couscous is tender
and liquid is absorbed. Transfer to a serving platter.
Spoon chicken mixture over couscous, and sprinkle
with pine nuts. Yield: 4 servings.

PER SERVING: 351 CALORIES (14% FROM FAT)
FAT 5.6G (SATURATED FAT 1.0G)
PROTEIN 28.5G   CARBOHYDRATE 48.6G
CHOLESTEROL 53MG   SODIUM 216MG

CHICKEN ADOBO WITH PEPPERS

2 tablespoons lime juice
1 tablespoon minced jalapeño pepper
2 teaspoons olive oil
1 clove garlic, minced
Dash of dried thyme
4 (4-ounce) skinned, boned chicken breast
    halves
Vegetable cooking spray
1 cup sliced green pepper
1 cup sliced sweet red pepper
Yellow Rice

Combine first 5 ingredients in a large, shallow
dish, and stir well. Add chicken, turning to coat.
Cover and marinate in refrigerator about 1½ hours,
turning chicken occasionally.

Coat a nonstick skillet with cooking spray; place
over medium-high heat until hot. Add peppers, and
sauté 3 minutes. Remove pepper from skillet; set
aside. Add chicken and marinade to skillet; cook
until chicken is lightly browned on both sides.
Return pepper to skillet; cover and cook over
medium heat about 5 minutes or until chicken is
done. Serve over Yellow Rice. Yield: 4 servings.

YELLOW RICE
1 teaspoon olive oil
1 cup uncooked long-grain rice
1 clove garlic, minced
⅛ teaspoon threads of saffron
2 cups canned no-salt-added chicken broth,
    undiluted
⅛ teaspoon salt

Heat oil in a saucepan over medium heat. Add
next 3 ingredients; sauté 2 minutes or until garlic is
tender. Stir in chicken broth and salt; bring to a
boil. Cover, reduce heat, and simmer 17 minutes or
until broth is absorbed. Yield: 4 (⅔-cup) servings.

PER SERVING: 366 CALORIES (16% FROM FAT)
FAT 6.6G (SATURATED FAT 1.3G)
PROTEIN 31.3G   CARBOHYDRATE 42.6G
CHOLESTEROL 66MG   SODIUM 216MG

Spicy Seafood Boil

SPICY SEAFOOD BOIL

2 pounds steamer clams
3 medium ears fresh corn
18 small round red potatoes (about 2¼ pounds)
3 large sweet onions, peeled
6 live blue crabs (about 3¼ pounds)
2 (3-ounce) packages crab boil
3 lemons, halved
2 cloves garlic, minced
1 cup vinegar
½ teaspoon freshly ground pepper
1½ pounds unpeeled medium-size fresh
   shrimp
Lemon wedges (optional)
Chile Mayonnaise

Scrub clams. Set aside.
Remove outer husks of corn; peel back light green husks. Remove silk, and replace husks. Secure husks to corn with string, and set aside.
Fill a 5-gallon pot about two-thirds full of water; bring to a boil. Add potatoes and onions; cover and cook over high heat 20 minutes. Stir in clams, crabs, and next 5 ingredients; cook an additional 10 minutes. Reduce heat, and add corn; simmer 5 minutes. Remove from heat, and add shrimp; let stand 5 minutes or until shrimp turn pink. Drain.
Cut corn and onions in half. Arrange boiled seafood and vegetables on a large serving platter. Garnish with lemon wedges, if desired. Serve with Chile Mayonnaise. Yield: 6 servings.

CHILE MAYONNAISE
½ cup reduced-calorie mayonnaise
½ cup soft tofu
1 small jalapeño pepper, seeded and halved
2 teaspoons red wine vinegar
1 teaspoon chili powder
1 teaspoon ground cumin

Position knife blade in food processor bowl; add mayonnaise and tofu. Process until smooth.
Place pepper, skin side up, on a baking sheet. Broil 5½ inches from heat 3 to 4 minutes or until pepper is blistered. Place in ice water, and chill 3 minutes. Remove pepper; peel and discard skin.

Add pepper and remaining ingredients to mayonnaise mixture; process 1 minute or until smooth, scraping sides of processor bowl once. Cover and chill. Yield: 1 cup.

PER SERVING: 375 CALORIES (19% FROM FAT)
FAT 8.0G (SATURATED FAT 1.2G)
PROTEIN 25.5G   CARBOHYDRATE 53.1G
CHOLESTEROL 128MG   SODIUM 463MG

CLAMS IN RED SAUCE

3 dozen littleneck clams
2 tablespoons cornmeal
Vegetable cooking spray
1 tablespoon olive oil
½ cup finely chopped onion
1 clove garlic, minced
1 cup Chablis or other dry white wine
2 (14-ounce) cans plum tomatoes with basil,
   undrained and chopped
2 (8-ounce) cans no-salt-added tomato sauce
1 tablespoon dried basil
½ teaspoon crushed red pepper
6 cups cooked linguine (cooked without salt
   or fat)
¼ cup chopped fresh parsley

Scrub clams. Place in a large bowl; cover with cold water, and sprinkle with cornmeal. Let stand 30 minutes. Drain; rinse clams. Discard cornmeal.
Coat a Dutch oven with cooking spray; add oil. Place over medium heat. Sauté onion and garlic until tender. Add wine; bring to a boil, and cook 5 minutes. Add tomato and next 3 ingredients; reduce heat, and simmer, uncovered, 10 minutes, stirring occasionally.
Place clams on top of tomato mixture. Cover and cook 8 to 10 minutes or until clams open. Remove and discard any unopened clams.
Divide linguine among 6 bowls; top with clam mixture. Sprinkle with parsley. Yield: 6 servings.

PER SERVING: 333 CALORIES (11% FROM FAT)
FAT 4.1G (SATURATED FAT 0.6G)
PROTEIN 16.6G   CARBOHYDRATE 57.3G
CHOLESTEROL 19MG   SODIUM 271MG

Cajun Gumbo and Rice

Cajun Gumbo and Rice

Instead of relying on a traditional fat-laden roux (a mixture consisting of half flour and half fat), this gumbo derives its rich flavor from an assortment of salt-free seasonings and its thickened consistency from gumbo filé.

1 tablespoon vegetable oil
1 cup chopped onion
1 cup chopped celery
¾ cup chopped green pepper
¾ cup chopped sweet red pepper
4 ounces Canadian bacon, chopped
2 cloves garlic, minced
2 (13¾-ounce) cans no-salt-added chicken broth
1 (14½-ounce) can no-salt-added whole tomatoes, undrained and chopped
¼ cup chopped fresh parsley
½ teaspoon salt
½ teaspoon dried basil
½ teaspoon dried thyme
¼ teaspoon ground red pepper
2 bay leaves
1 (10-ounce) package frozen sliced okra, thawed
1 tablespoon plus 1 teaspoon cornstarch
¼ cup water
2 pounds medium-size fresh shrimp, peeled and deveined
2 tablespoons gumbo filé
4½ cups cooked long-grain rice (cooked without salt or fat)
Hot sauce (optional)

Heat oil in a Dutch oven over medium-high heat until hot. Add onion, celery, green pepper, sweet red pepper, Canadian bacon, and garlic; sauté until tender. Add chicken broth and next 7 ingredients, stirring well. Bring to a boil. Cover, reduce heat, and simmer 20 minutes.

Stir okra into vegetable mixture; cover and cook 5 minutes. Combine cornstarch and water; add to hot mixture. Stir in shrimp and filé; cook 5 minutes or until shrimp turn pink. Remove and discard bay leaves.

To serve, ladle 1 cup gumbo over ½ cup serving of rice; sprinkle with hot sauce, if desired. Yield: 9 servings.

PER SERVING: 319 CALORIES (18% FROM FAT)
FAT 6.5G (SATURATED FAT 1.2G)
PROTEIN 23.3G   CARBOHYDRATE 40.2G
CHOLESTEROL 121MG   SODIUM 496MG

Seafood and Pasta in Chunky Tomato Sauce

Peel and devein the shrimp a day ahead, and cook the pasta an hour early. The rest of the recipe is a snap to put together.

1 pound unpeeled medium-size fresh shrimp
1 teaspoon olive oil
2 cloves garlic, minced
1 pound sea scallops, halved
⅓ cup Chablis or other dry white wine
½ teaspoon crushed red pepper
1 (25½-ounce) jar nonfat chunky Italian-style vegetable pasta sauce
6 cups cooked rigatoni (short tubular pasta), cooked without salt or fat
¼ cup grated Asiago or Parmesan cheese
¼ cup tightly packed, thinly sliced fresh basil or chopped fresh parsley

Peel and devein shrimp.

Heat olive oil in a large saucepan over medium heat. Add minced garlic, and sauté 1 minute. Add shrimp, scallops, and next 3 ingredients. Cook 10 minutes or until shrimp and scallops are done, stirring occasionally.

Combine the sauce mixture and pasta in a large shallow bowl, and stir gently. Sprinkle with grated Asiago cheese and basil. Yield: 6 (1½-cup) servings.

PER SERVING: 362 CALORIES (11% FROM FAT)
FAT 4.3G (SATURATED FAT 1.2G)
PROTEIN 35.6G   CARBOHYDRATE 42.6G
CHOLESTEROL 142MG   SODIUM 671MG

CREOLE CATFISH

¼ cup clam juice
¼ cup water
1 cup chopped onion
1 cup chopped celery
½ cup chopped green pepper
2 teaspoons minced garlic
1 (14½-ounce) can no-salt-added whole
    tomatoes, undrained and pureed
¼ pound fresh mushrooms, chopped
¼ cup Chablis or other dry white wine
2 tablespoons lemon juice
1 tablespoon low-sodium Worcestershire sauce
½ teaspoon sugar
¼ teaspoon black pepper
⅛ teaspoon ground red pepper
4 drops of hot sauce
2 bay leaves
1 pound farm-raised catfish fillets
3 cups cooked long-grain rice (cooked without
    salt or fat)

Combine first 6 ingredients in a medium saucepan; bring to a boil. Cover, reduce heat, and simmer 10 minutes. Stir in tomato and next 9 ingredients. Bring to a boil; cover, reduce heat, and simmer 20 minutes.

Cut fillets into 1½-inch pieces; add to tomato mixture. Cook, uncovered, 10 minutes or until fish flakes easily when tested with a fork, stirring occasionally. Remove and discard bay leaves.

To serve, spoon 1 cup catfish mixture over ½ cup rice. Yield: 6 servings.

PER SERVING: 253 CALORIES (13% FROM FAT)
FAT 3.7G (SATURATED FAT 0.9G)
PROTEIN 18.0G   CARBOHYDRATE 36.3G
CHOLESTEROL 44MG   SODIUM 110MG

CREOLE BLACK-EYED PEAS AND POLENTA

5 cups water, divided
¾ teaspoon salt
¾ cup instant polenta
¼ cup freshly grated Parmesan cheese
Vegetable cooking spray
3½ cups frozen black-eyed peas
1¼ cups chopped onion
1¼ cups chopped green pepper
2 cloves garlic, minced
2 (14½-ounce) cans no-salt-added stewed
    tomatoes, undrained and chopped
1 tablespoon low-sodium Worcestershire sauce
½ teaspoon salt
¼ teaspoon ground red pepper
¼ teaspoon black pepper
¼ teaspoon hot sauce
Fresh parsley sprigs (optional)

Combine 3 cups water and ¾ teaspoon salt in a medium saucepan; bring to a boil. Add polenta in a slow, steady stream, stirring constantly. Reduce heat to medium, and cook 20 minutes, stirring constantly, or until mixture pulls away from sides of pan. Add cheese, stirring until cheese melts. Spoon mixture into a 9- x 5- x 3-inch loafpan coated with cooking spray. Set aside, and let cool completely.

Combine peas and remaining 2 cups water in a large saucepan. Bring to a boil; cover, reduce heat, and simmer 20 minutes. Drain and set aside.

Coat a nonstick skillet with cooking spray; place over medium heat until hot. Add onion, green pepper, and garlic; sauté until tender. Stir in peas, tomato, and next 5 ingredients; bring mixture to a boil. Reduce heat; simmer, uncovered, 10 minutes or until peas are tender, stirring occasionally.

Turn polenta out onto a cutting board; cut crosswise into 18 (½-inch) slices. Arrange 3 slices on each of 6 plates; top with 1 cup pea mixture. Garnish with parsley, if desired. Yield: 6 servings.

PER SERVING: 274 CALORIES (8% FROM FAT)
FAT 2.5G (SATURATED FAT 1.0G)
PROTEIN 14.2G   CARBOHYDRATE 50.3G
CHOLESTEROL 3MG   SODIUM 601MG

Creole Black-Eyed Peas and Polenta

Polenta, a cornmeal-based mixture that originated in northern Italy, is done when it pulls away from the sides of the pan and forms a ball.

Press the cooked polenta mixture into a loafpan that has been coated with vegetable cooking spray. A flexible rubber spatula makes this an easy task.

After it cools, turn out the polenta onto a cutting board, and cut into 1/2-inch slices. Each serving consists of 3 slices of polenta topped with 1 cup pea mixture.

SPICY RED BEANS AND CHUNKY RICE

¾ pound dried red kidney beans
2 cups water
Vegetable cooking spray
1½ tablespoons vegetable oil
1¼ cups chopped onion
2 cloves garlic, minced
2½ cups water
2 bay leaves
1 tablespoon beef-flavored bouillon granules
½ teaspoon dried oregano
½ teaspoon hot sauce
1 tablespoon honey
Chunky Rice
Fresh oregano sprigs (optional)

Sort and wash beans. Place beans and 2 cups water in a medium saucepan; bring to a boil. Cover, remove from heat, and let stand 1 hour. Drain beans, and set aside.

Coat a large Dutch oven with cooking spray; add oil. Place over medium-high heat until hot. Add onion and garlic, and sauté until tender. Add beans, 2½ cups water, and next 5 ingredients; bring to a boil. Cover, reduce heat, and simmer 2 hours or until beans are tender.

Remove pan from heat, and discard bay leaves. Serve over Chunky Rice. Garnish with oregano sprigs, if desired. Yield: 8 servings.

Spicy Red Beans and Chunky Rice

CHUNKY RICE

Vegetable cooking spray
1 cup chopped onion
1 cup finely chopped carrot
1 cup finely chopped celery
¾ cup finely chopped sweet red pepper
½ cup finely chopped green pepper
2 cloves garlic, minced
1⅓ cups uncooked long-grain rice
1 teaspoon Cajun seasoning
2 tablespoons chopped fresh parsley

Coat a large nonstick skillet with cooking spray; place over medium-high heat until hot. Add onion and next 5 ingredients, and sauté until tender. Set aside.

Cook rice according to package directions, omitting salt and fat; add 1 teaspoon Cajun seasoning. Toss vegetables, rice, and parsley. Yield: 4 cups.

PER SERVING: 324 CALORIES (10% FROM FAT)
FAT 3.7G (SATURATED FAT 0.7G)
PROTEIN 13.4G   CARBOHYDRATE 60.3G
CHOLESTEROL 0MG   SODIUM 419MG

Did You Know?

Both Creole and Cajun cooking have swept the country but still have their roots in southern Louisiana. Although the French influence is strong in each of these cuisines, Creole dishes use ample amounts of butter and cream, while Cajun cooking depends on herbs, seasonings, and spices to bring out the full flavor of the main ingredients.

POTATO-CHILE OMELET

1½ cups diced unpeeled round red potato
½ teaspoon vegetable oil
⅓ cup thinly sliced green onions
3 tablespoons chopped green chiles, drained
½ teaspoon chili powder
¼ teaspoon garlic powder
⅛ teaspoon ground red pepper
2 egg yolks
1 tablespoon skim milk
3 egg whites
1 tablespoon all-purpose flour
½ teaspoon sugar
¼ teaspoon salt
¼ teaspoon black pepper
Vegetable cooking spray
¼ cup seeded, chopped unpeeled tomato
2 tablespoons commercial mild salsa

Combine potato and water to cover in a saucepan; bring to a boil. Reduce heat; simmer 10 minutes or until tender. Drain well; set aside.

Heat oil in a small nonstick skillet over medium high heat until hot; add green onions and chiles, and sauté 2 minutes. Add potato, and cook 3 minutes or until potato is lightly browned. Stir in chili powder and next 2 ingredients; remove from heat, and set aside.

Beat egg yolks in a bowl until thick and pale (about 5 minutes). Add milk; beat until blended.

Beat egg whites (at room temperature) until soft peaks form; add flour and next 3 ingredients. Beat until stiff peaks form. Fold into egg yolks.

Coat a 10-inch nonstick skillet with cooking spray, and place over medium heat until hot. Spread egg mixture evenly into skillet. Top with potato mixture. Cover, reduce heat to medium-low, and cook 15 minutes or until center is set. Combine tomato and salsa; spoon over half of omelet. Loosen omelet with a spatula, and fold in half. Slide omelet onto a serving plate; cut in half. Yield: 2 servings.

PER SERVING: 231 CALORIES (28% FROM FAT)
FAT 7.2G (SATURATED FAT 1.9G)
PROTEIN 12.0G   CARBOHYDRATE 30.6G
CHOLESTEROL 218MG   SODIUM 468MG

MEALS FROM THE OVEN

*H*ave you ever gone stir-crazy in the kitchen? Then take a break with these main-dish recipes. The ingredients go into the dish, into the oven, and onto the table. You won't have to lift a hand to stir during cooking.

To further simplify meal preparation, assemble these dishes ahead and store in the refrigerator or freezer until needed. Hearty dishes such as Onion-Topped Pot Roast (page 102) often keep well and may taste even better after reheating because the flavors will have blended. If you freeze an unbaked casserole, defrost it in the refrigerator or microwave oven, and then bake as directed.

Pesto-Stuffed Shells (Recipe follows on page 119)

Onion-Topped Pot Roast

ONION-TOPPED POT ROAST

1 (2-pound) lean, boneless bottom round roast
Vegetable cooking spray
¼ teaspoon pepper
2 cloves garlic
1 cup coarsely chopped onion
½ cup Burgundy or other dry red wine
½ cup canned no-salt-added beef broth, undiluted
¼ cup no-salt-added tomato juice
½ teaspoon salt
1 cup water
18 small unpeeled round red potatoes (about 1½ pounds)
18 baby carrots (about ½ pound)

Trim fat from roast. Coat a Dutch oven with cooking spray; place over medium-high heat until hot. Add roast, and cook until browned on all sides. Remove roast from pan, and sprinkle with pepper; set roast aside. Wipe drippings from pan with a paper towel.

Position knife blade in food processor bowl. With food processor running, drop garlic through food chute, and process 5 seconds. Add chopped onion, and process about 1 minute or until mixture is smooth. Spread onion puree evenly over roast. Return roast to Dutch oven. Bake, uncovered, at 350° for 1 hour.

Add wine and next 3 ingredients to pan. Cover and bake 2½ hours. Add water, potatoes, and carrots; cover and bake an additional hour or until roast is tender.

Place meat and vegetables on a platter; serve with gravy. Yield: 6 servings.

PER SERVING: 293 CALORIES (17% FROM FAT)
FAT 5.6G (SATURATED FAT 2.0G)
PROTEIN 33.1G   CARBOHYDRATE 26.4G
CHOLESTEROL 74MG   SODIUM 288MG

SPINACH-BEEF LASAGNA

Vegetable cooking spray
1 pound ground round
½ cup chopped onion
1 (30¾-ounce) jar no-salt-added spaghetti
 sauce
1½ cups water
¼ teaspoon salt
2 (10-ounce) packages frozen chopped
 spinach, thawed
1 (15-ounce) carton nonfat ricotta cheese
1 cup (4 ounces) shredded part-skim
 mozzarella cheese, divided
½ cup frozen egg substitute, thawed
1 (2-ounce) jar diced pimiento, drained
9 lasagna noodles, uncooked

Coat a large nonstick skillet with cooking spray;
place over medium-high heat until hot. Cook
ground round and onion over medium heat until
browned, stirring until meat crumbles. Drain and
pat dry with paper towels. Wipe drippings from
skillet with a paper towel.

Return meat mixture to skillet. Add spaghetti
sauce, water, and salt; bring to a boil. Reduce heat
and simmer, uncovered, 10 minutes; set aside.

Drain spinach; press between paper towels.
Combine ricotta cheese, ½ cup mozzarella cheese,
egg substitute, and pimiento; stir in spinach.

Coat a 13- x 9- x 2-inch baking dish with cooking
spray. Spoon 1 cup meat mixture into dish. Place 3
uncooked lasagna noodles over meat mixture.
Spoon one-third of remaining meat mixture over
noodles; top with half of spinach mixture. Place 3
lasagna noodles over spinach mixture; spoon half of
remaining beef mixture over noodles. Top with
remaining spinach mixture. Top with remaining 3
noodles and remaining meat mixture.

Cover and bake at 350° for 55 minutes. Uncover;
sprinkle with remaining ½ cup mozzarella cheese.
Bake, uncovered, 5 minutes or until cheese melts.
Let stand 10 minutes; serve. Yield: 10 servings.

PER SERVING: 306 CALORIES (22% FROM FAT)
FAT 7.5G (SATURATED FAT 2.5G)
PROTEIN 26.3G   CARBOHYDRATE 36.6G
CHOLESTEROL 39MG   SODIUM 241MG

PIZZA-STYLE STUFFED PEPPERS

4 large green peppers
¾ pound ground round
1 cup fresh mushrooms, chopped
¾ cup chopped onion
1 cup no-salt-added meatless spaghetti sauce
2 tablespoons water
1 teaspoon dried Italian seasoning
¼ teaspoon salt
¼ teaspoon pepper
2 cups cooked long-grain rice (cooked without
 salt or fat)
½ cup (2 ounces) shredded part-skim
 mozzarella cheese

Cut tops off green peppers, and remove seeds.
Trim stem from tops and discard. Chop remaining
green pepper tops; set aside. Arrange pepper shells
in a vegetable steamer over boiling water. Cover
and steam 5 minutes. Drain shells, and set aside.

Combine ground round, mushrooms, onion, and
reserved chopped green pepper in a large nonstick
skillet; cook over medium heat until beef is
browned, stirring until it crumbles. Drain and pat
dry with paper towels. Wipe drippings from skillet
with a paper towel.

Return meat mixture to skillet; add spaghetti
sauce and next 4 ingredients. Bring to a boil;
reduce heat, and simmer 5 minutes. Stir in rice.
Spoon beef mixture evenly into shells; place shells
in an 8-inch square baking dish. Pour hot water
into baking dish to a depth of 1 inch. Bake at 350°
for 15 to 20 minutes; sprinkle evenly with cheese,
and bake an additional 5 minutes or until cheese
melts. Yield: 4 servings.

PER SERVING: 392 CALORIES (22% FROM FAT)
FAT 9.6G (SATURATED FAT 3.3G)
PROTEIN 27.9G   CARBOHYDRATE 50.0G
CHOLESTEROL 61MG   SODIUM 274MG

Hearty Shepherd's Pie

HEARTY SHEPHERD'S PIE

4½ cups peeled, cubed baking potato
⅓ cup skim milk
¼ cup grated Parmesan cheese
2 tablespoons reduced-calorie margarine
⅛ teaspoon salt
1½ pounds ground round
1 cup sliced carrot
1 cup coarsely chopped onion
½ cup chopped green pepper
1 large clove garlic, minced
2 teaspoons low-sodium Worcestershire sauce
1 teaspoon dried basil
½ teaspoon salt
½ teaspoon dried oregano
¼ teaspoon pepper
1 (14½-ounce) can no-salt-added whole
    tomatoes, undrained and chopped
1 bay leaf
2 tablespoons all-purpose flour
2 tablespoons water
1 cup frozen English peas, thawed

Cook potato in boiling water to cover 15 minutes or until tender; drain. Combine potato and next 4 ingredients in a bowl; beat at medium speed of an electric mixer 2 minutes or until smooth. Set aside.

Cook ground round in a large nonstick skillet over medium heat until browned, stirring until it crumbles. Drain well, and set aside. Wipe drippings from skillet. Add carrot and next 3 ingredients to skillet; sauté over medium heat 5 minutes or until crisp-tender.

Return meat to skillet. Add Worcestershire sauce and next 6 ingredients; bring to a boil. Cover, reduce heat, and simmer 30 minutes. Remove from heat; discard bay leaf. Place flour in a bowl; gradually add 2 tablespoons water, stirring with a wire whisk. Add to meat mixture; stir well. Stir in peas.

Spoon meat into a 3-quart casserole coated with cooking spray. Spoon potato mixture over meat, spreading to edges. Bake at 350° for 40 minutes; let stand 10 minutes. Yield: 6 (1⅔-cup) servings.

PER SERVING: 363 CALORIES (27% FROM FAT)
FAT 10.7G (SATURATED FAT 3.5G)
PROTEIN 31.2G   CARBOHYDRATE 35.0G
CHOLESTEROL 73MG   SODIUM 463MG

MUSHROOM-VEAL ROULADES

6 (4-ounce) veal cutlets (¼ inch thick)
2½ cups chopped fresh mushrooms
½ cup chopped onion
2 tablespoons chopped fresh parsley
1 teaspoon no-salt-added herb salad seasoning
¼ teaspoon coarsely ground pepper
2 teaspoons low-sodium soy sauce
1 cup hot water
1 teaspoon beef-flavored bouillon granules
Vegetable cooking spray
3 tablespoons all-purpose flour
¼ cup dry sherry
¼ teaspoon salt
⅛ teaspoon pepper
½ cup low-fat sour cream
3 cups cooked medium egg noodles (cooked
    without salt or fat)

Trim fat from cutlets. Place cutlets between 2 sheets of heavy-duty plastic wrap; flatten to ⅛-inch thickness, using a meat mallet or rolling pin.

Combine mushrooms and next 4 ingredients. Spoon ¼ cup mixture onto center of each cutlet. Reserve remaining mixture. Roll up cutlets, jelly-roll fashion, starting at short side. Secure with wooden picks. Place rolls in a 9-inch square baking dish; brush with soy sauce.

Combine water and bouillon granules; pour around rolls. Cover and bake at 350° for 30 minutes or until veal is tender. Remove from dish, using a slotted spoon. Reserve bouillon mixture.

Coat a skillet with cooking spray; place over medium heat until hot. Add reserved mushroom mixture; sauté until tender. Stir in flour. Add bouillon mixture. Cook over medium heat, stirring constantly, until thickened and bubbly. Stir in sherry, salt, and pepper. Remove from heat; let stand 1 minute. Stir in sour cream. Add veal to mushroom sauce. Serve over noodles. Yield: 6 servings.

PER SERVING: 296 CALORIES (22% FROM FAT)
FAT 7.3G (SATURATED FAT 2.8G)
PROTEIN 28.7G   CARBOHYDRATE 27.4G
CHOLESTEROL 128MG   SODIUM 411MG

Marinated Veal Roast

MARINATED VEAL ROAST

1 (3½-pound) boneless rolled veal rump roast
Buttermilk Marinade
1 teaspoon dried thyme
½ teaspoon pepper
Vegetable cooking spray
28 small round red potatoes
28 small boiling onions
6 large carrots, cut into thick strips
2 teaspoons vegetable oil
Fresh parsley sprigs (optional)
Fresh thyme sprigs (optional)

Unroll roast; trim fat from roast. Roll roast; tie securely at 2-inch intervals with string. Place in a large heavy-duty, zip-top plastic bag. Add half of Buttermilk Marinade. Cover and refrigerate remaining marinade. Seal plastic bag; marinate roast in refrigerator 8 hours, turning occasionally.

Remove roast from marinade, and discard marinade. Pat roast dry with paper towels, and sprinkle with dried thyme and pepper. Place roast in a shallow roasting pan coated with cooking spray. Insert meat thermometer into thickest portion of roast.

Cook potatoes in boiling water to cover in a large Dutch oven 5 minutes; add onions and carrot. Cook an additional 3 minutes; drain. Place vegetables in a large bowl; add oil, and toss gently.

Arrange vegetables around roast in pan. Bake, uncovered, at 450° for 20 minutes. Reduce heat to 325°; cover and bake an additional 45 to 50 minutes or until meat thermometer registers 160° (medium), stirring vegetables once. Transfer roast and vegetables to a large serving platter, discarding pan drippings. Remove string from roast. If desired, garnish with parsley and thyme. Serve with reserved Buttermilk Marinade. Yield: 14 servings.

BUTTERMILK MARINADE

2 cups nonfat buttermilk
1 (8-ounce) carton low-fat sour cream
½ cup nonfat mayonnaise
3 tablespoons chopped fresh parsley
2 tablespoons grated Parmesan cheese
½ teaspoon garlic powder
½ teaspoon onion powder
⅛ teaspoon dry mustard

Combine all ingredients in a medium bowl; stir well. Yield. 3¾ cups.

PER SERVING: 245 CALORIES (15% FROM FAT)
FAT 4.0G (SATURATED FAT 1.5G)
PROTEIN 27.8G   CARBOHYDRATE 23.8G
CHOLESTEROL 92MG   SODIUM 177MG

CHICKEN-RICE ITALIANO

1½ cups water
1 cup long-grain rice, uncooked
½ cup chopped onion
½ cup (2 ounces) shredded part-skim
   mozzarella cheese
1½ teaspoons dried Italian seasoning
½ teaspoon salt-free garlic-and-herb spice
   blend
¼ teaspoon salt
¼ teaspoon pepper
1 (14½-ounce) can no-salt-added whole
   tomatoes, undrained and chopped
Vegetable cooking spray
4 (4-ounce) skinned, boned chicken breast
   halves
½ teaspoon garlic powder
½ cup grated Parmesan cheese
1½ teaspoons dried Italian seasoning

Combine first 9 ingredients in a 2-quart casserole coated with cooking spray, and stir well.

Arrange chicken breast halves over rice mixture, and sprinkle with garlic powder. Sprinkle with Parmesan cheese and 1½ teaspoons Italian seasoning. Cover and bake at 375° for 45 minutes. Uncover and bake an additional 15 minutes or until liquid is absorbed. Yield: 4 servings.

PER SERVING: 431 CALORIES (20% FROM FAT)
FAT 9.7G (SATURATED FAT 4.8G)
PROTEIN 38.0G   CARBOHYDRATE 45.7G
CHOLESTEROL 91MG   SODIUM 465MG

SWEET-AND-SOUR CHICKEN-STUFFED PEPPERS

1 medium-size sweet yellow pepper
1 (8-ounce) can unsweetened pineapple
    chunks, undrained
Vegetable cooking spray
1 cup chopped cooked chicken breast (about
    ½ pound skinned, boned chicken breasts)
½ cup diagonally sliced green onions
½ cup diagonally sliced carrot
½ cup diced unpeeled tomato
1 tablespoon cornstarch
1 tablespoon brown sugar
2 tablespoons cider vinegar
1 teaspoon low-sodium soy sauce
1 cup cooked long-grain rice (cooked without
    salt or fat)

Cut pepper in half lengthwise. Discard seeds
and membranes. Cook pepper halves in boiling
water to cover 4 minutes. Drain pepper halves, and
set aside.

Drain pineapple chunks, reserving juice; set
pineapple juice aside.

Coat a medium skillet with cooking spray; place
over medium heat until hot. Add chicken, green
onions, carrot, and tomato; cook 5 minutes or until
carrot is tender.

Combine reserved pineapple juice, cornstarch,
and next 3 ingredients in a bowl; stir well. Add
pineapple chunks and cornstarch mixture to chick-
en mixture; cook 3 minutes or until thickened, stirring mixture constantly.

Spoon half of chicken mixture into each pepper
half; place in a baking dish. Cover and bake at 350°
for 20 minutes or until thoroughly heated. Serve
over rice. Yield: 2 servings.

PER SERVING: 396 CALORIES (9% FROM FAT)
FAT 3.9G (SATURATED FAT 0.9G)
PROTEIN 29.8G   CARBOHYDRATE 59.0G
CHOLESTEROL 72MG   SODIUM 150MG

CHICKEN WITH ROASTED PEARS AND WILD RICE

1 cup wild rice, uncooked
2 cups unsweetened apple juice
1 cup water
1 pound skinned, boned chicken breasts, cut
    into bite-size pieces
½ cup dried cranberries or dried tart cherries
2 teaspoons sugar
½ teaspoon salt
½ teaspoon ground cinnamon
2 small, firm unpeeled ripe Bosc pears (about
    ¾ pound), cored and cut lengthwise into
    ½-inch-thick slices
Vegetable cooking spray

Combine rice, apple juice, and water in a medium saucepan; bring to a boil. Cover, reduce heat,
and simmer about 1 hour or until liquid is absorbed
and rice is tender; drain.

Combine rice, chicken, and next 4 ingredients in
a bowl; stir well. Spoon mixture into an 11- x 7- x
2-inch baking dish; set aside.

Arrange pear slices in a single layer on a baking
sheet coated with cooking spray. Bake pear slices at
450° for 10 minutes or until tender.

Arrange roasted pear slices over the chicken mixture. Cover and bake at 400° for 30 minutes or until
chicken is done. Yield: 4 (1½-cup) servings.

PER SERVING: 403 CALORIES (6% FROM FAT)
FAT 2.5G (SATURATED FAT 0.5G)
PROTEIN 32.5G   CARBOHYDRATE 64.0G
CHOLESTEROL 66MG   SODIUM 373MG

CHICKEN, ARTICHOKE, AND WILD RICE CASSEROLE

1 (6-ounce) package wild rice, cooked without salt or fat
½ teaspoon salt, divided
¼ teaspoon paprika
¼ teaspoon pepper
6 (4-ounce) skinned, boned chicken breast halves
Vegetable cooking spray
1 tablespoon margarine
1 (14-ounce) can artichoke hearts, drained and cut in half
3⅓ cups sliced fresh mushrooms
3 tablespoons plus 2 teaspoons all-purpose flour
½ teaspoon dried rosemary, crushed
2¼ cups canned low-sodium chicken broth, undiluted
½ cup dry sherry

Spoon wild rice into an 11- x 7- x 2-inch baking dish; set aside. Sprinkle ¼ teaspoon salt, paprika, and pepper over chicken; set aside.

Coat a large nonstick skillet with cooking spray; add margarine, and place over medium heat until margarine melts. Add chicken, and cook 4 minutes on each side. Arrange chicken on top of rice; top with artichoke hearts, and set aside.

Add mushrooms to skillet, and sauté over medium heat 5 minutes. Combine remaining ¼ teaspoon salt, flour, and remaining ingredients; stir well. Add to skillet; cook 3 minutes, stirring constantly, or until thickened and bubbly. Spoon over chicken. Cover and bake at 375° for 55 minutes or until thoroughly heated. Yield: 6 servings.

PER SERVING: 311 CALORIES (13% FROM FAT)
FAT 4.6G (SATURATED FAT 0.9G)
PROTEIN 33.8G   CARBOHYDRATE 34.1G
CHOLESTEROL 66MG   SODIUM 370MG

Chicken, Artichoke, and Wild Rice Casserole

Chicken-Vegetable Pot Pies

CHICKEN-VEGETABLE POT PIES

3 (6-ounce) skinned chicken breast halves
2½ cups water
2 medium baking potatoes, peeled and cut into
   ½-inch cubes
½ cup chopped celery
1 teaspoon chicken-flavored bouillon granules
1 (10-ounce) package frozen mixed vegetables
2 tablespoons margarine
2 tablespoons all-purpose flour
1 cup skim milk
1 teaspoon poultry seasoning
1 (4-ounce) can sliced mushrooms, drained
Vegetable cooking spray
1 cup all-purpose flour
1 teaspoon baking powder
¼ teaspoon salt
1½ tablespoons margarine
½ cup nonfat buttermilk
Celery leaves (optional)

Combine chicken and water in a large saucepan.
Bring to a boil; cover, reduce heat, and simmer 30
minutes or until chicken is tender. Remove
chicken from broth. Bone chicken, and cut into
bite-size pieces; set aside. Skim and discard fat
from broth.

Add potato, celery, and bouillon granules to
broth. Bring to a boil; cover, reduce heat, and simmer 15 minutes or until potato is tender. Stir in
mixed vegetables; remove from heat, and set aside.

Melt 2 tablespoons margarine in a saucepan over
medium heat; add 2 tablespoons flour, stirring until
smooth. Cook 1 minute, stirring constantly.
Gradually add milk, stirring constantly. Cook, stirring constantly, until mixture is thickened and bubbly. Remove from heat; stir in poultry seasoning.

Add chicken, vegetable mixture, and mushrooms
to saucepan. Spoon chicken mixture into each of 6
(1-cup) baking dishes coated with cooking spray.

Combine 1 cup flour, baking powder, and salt in
a small bowl. Cut in 1½ tablespoons margarine
with a pastry blender until mixture resembles
coarse meal. Add buttermilk, stirring just until dry
ingredients are moistened. Drop dough evenly by
tablespoonfuls onto chicken mixture. Bake at 350°
for 45 minutes or until crusts are golden. Garnish
with celery leaves, if desired. Yield: 6 servings.

PER SERVING: 322 CALORIES (25% FROM FAT)
FAT 9.1G (SATURATED FAT 1.9G)
PROTEIN 20.4G CARBOHYDRATE 39.6G
CHOLESTEROL 36MG SODIUM 437MG

EASY CHICKEN POT PIES

Vegetable cooking spray
1 cup diced carrot
1 cup sliced fresh mushrooms
½ cup chopped celery
½ cup frozen English peas, thawed
¼ cup minced onion
1½ (10¾-ounce) cans one-third-less-salt
   cream of chicken soup, undiluted
1½ cups water
½ teaspoon pepper
¼ teaspoon dried thyme
3 cups diced cooked chicken breast
1 cup self-rising flour
1½ tablespoons margarine
¼ cup skim milk

Coat a large nonstick skillet with cooking spray;
place over medium-high heat until hot. Add carrot,
mushrooms, celery, peas, and onion. Sauté 5 minutes or until vegetables are tender.

Combine soup, water, pepper, and thyme in a
medium bowl; stir well. Add vegetables and cooked
chicken, stirring well.

Spoon chicken mixture evenly into 6 (8-ounce)
round baking dishes coated with cooking spray.

Place flour in a small bowl; cut in margarine with
a pastry blender until mixture is crumbly. Sprinkle
milk, 1 tablespoon at a time, evenly over surface,
stirring with a fork until dry ingredients are moistened. Drop dough evenly by tablespoonfuls onto
chicken mixture. Bake at 425° for 15 to 18 minutes
or until crusts are golden. Yield: 6 servings.

PER SERVING: 281 CALORIES (22% FROM FAT)
FAT 6.8G (SATURATED FAT 1.5G)
PROTEIN 24.7G CARBOHYDRATE 28.5G
CHOLESTEROL 61MG SODIUM 716MG

Harvest Cornbread Chicken Pie

1 (3-pound) broiler-fryer, skinned
3 quarts water
2 cups peeled, cubed sweet potato
1 tablespoon cornstarch
1 tablespoon water
Vegetable cooking spray
1 cup chopped onion
1 cup frozen whole kernel corn, thawed
2 cloves garlic, minced
¾ cup self-rising flour
¾ cup self-rising cornmeal
1 teaspoon sugar
¾ teaspoon chili powder
¾ cup nonfat buttermilk
1 egg, lightly beaten

Place broiler-fryer and 3 quarts water in a Dutch oven. Bring to a boil; cover, reduce heat, and simmer 45 minutes or until chicken is tender. Remove chicken from broth, reserving broth. Let chicken cool to touch. Bone and chop chicken. Return chopped chicken to broth; cover and chill 8 hours.

Skim and discard fat from broth. Remove chicken with a slotted spoon; set aside. Bring broth to a boil; cook, uncovered, 50 minutes or until reduced by half. Add sweet potato, and cook, uncovered, 13 minutes or until tender; remove with a slotted spoon. Set sweet potato aside. Cook broth, uncovered, 20 minutes or until reduced to 1 cup.

Combine cornstarch and 1 tablespoon water; stir well. Add to broth; cook, stirring constantly, until thickened and bubbly.

Coat a large nonstick skillet with cooking spray; place over medium-high heat until hot. Add onion, corn, and garlic; sauté until tender. Add chicken, sweet potato, and broth mixture; stir well. Spoon mixture into an 11- x 7- x 2-inch baking dish coated with cooking spray. Set aside.

Combine flour, cornmeal, sugar, and chili powder in a bowl; make a well in center of mixture.

Combine buttermilk and egg; add to dry ingredients, stirring just until moistened. Spoon cornmeal batter evenly over chicken mixture. Bake at 425° for 15 minutes or until golden. Let stand 5 minutes before serving. Yield: 8 servings.

PER SERVING: 310 CALORIES (18% FROM FAT)
FAT 6.2G (SATURATED FAT 1.6G)
PROTEIN 23.5G   CARBOHYDRATE 36.3G
CHOLESTEROL 83MG   SODIUM 391MG

Baked Turkey Pastrami Casserole

1 (7-ounce) package vermicelli, uncooked
Vegetable cooking spray
1 tablespoon olive oil
1 medium onion, chopped
1 medium-size green pepper, seeded and chopped
½ pound fresh mushrooms, sliced
1 (8-ounce) package turkey pastrami, cut into thin strips
1 (16-ounce) jar no-salt-added meatless spaghetti sauce
¾ cup Chablis or other dry white wine
2 teaspoons dried Italian seasoning
1 cup (4 ounces) shredded part-skim mozzarella cheese

Cook pasta according to package directions, omitting salt and fat; drain.

Coat a large nonstick skillet with cooking spray; add oil. Place over medium-high heat until hot; add onion and green pepper, and sauté until tender. Add mushrooms and pastrami; cook over medium heat until thoroughly heated, stirring occasionally. Remove from heat; stir in cooked pasta, spaghetti sauce, wine, and Italian seasoning.

Spoon pasta mixture into a 13- x 9- x 2-inch baking dish coated with cooking spray. Cover and bake at 350° for 25 minutes. Sprinkle with cheese; bake, uncovered, an additional 5 minutes or until cheese melts. Yield: 8 servings.

PER SERVING: 251 CALORIES (27% FROM FAT)
FAT 7.4G (SATURATED FAT 2.2G)
PROTEIN 14.5G   CARBOHYDRATE 33.0G
CHOLESTEROL 26MG   SODIUM 369MG

Turkey Tetrazzini

TURKEY TETRAZZINI

1 (7-ounce) package spaghetti, uncooked
Vegetable cooking spray
1 tablespoon reduced-calorie margarine
3 cups sliced fresh mushrooms
⅓ cup minced onion
¼ cup diced celery
½ cup all-purpose flour
1½ cups skim milk
1 (13¾-ounce) can no-salt-added chicken broth
¼ cup light process cream cheese product
¼ cup grated Parmesan cheese, divided
¼ cup dry sherry
½ teaspoon salt
½ teaspoon garlic powder
¼ teaspoon pepper
1 (2-ounce) jar diced pimiento, drained
2 cups chopped cooked turkey breast

Break spaghetti in half. Cook according to package directions, omitting salt and fat; drain.

Coat a large saucepan with cooking spray; add margarine. Place over medium-high heat until margarine melts. Add mushrooms, onion, and celery; sauté until tender. Combine flour and milk, stirring until smooth. Add flour mixture and broth to vegetables. Bring to a boil over medium heat; reduce heat, and simmer 5 minutes, stirring constantly.

Remove from heat; add cream cheese, stirring until cheese melts. Stir in spaghetti, 2 tablespoons Parmesan cheese, and remaining ingredients.

Spoon turkey mixture into a shallow 2-quart baking dish coated with cooking spray; sprinkle with remaining 2 tablespoons Parmesan cheese. Bake at 350° for 25 to 30 minutes. Yield: 6 servings.

PER SERVING: 336 CALORIES (18% FROM FAT)
FAT 6.9G (SATURATED FAT 2.6G)
PROTEIN 25.8G   CARBOHYDRATE 41.2G
CHOLESTEROL 41MG   SODIUM 449MG

Turkey Chili Cobbler

TURKEY CHILI COBBLER

Vegetable cooking spray
1½ pounds ground turkey
1 cup chopped onion
1 medium-size green pepper, cored, seeded,
    and chopped
2 large cloves garlic, minced
2 (14½-ounce) cans no-salt-added whole
    tomatoes, undrained and coarsely chopped
1 (16-ounce) can red kidney beans, drained
1 (10-ounce) can diced tomatoes and green
    chiles, undrained
½ cup water
1½ tablespoons chili powder
1 teaspoon ground cumin
½ teaspoon freshly ground pepper
Cornbread Dumplings

Coat a Dutch oven with cooking spray; place over medium-high heat until hot. Add turkey, onion, green pepper, and garlic. Cook until turkey is browned, stirring until turkey crumbles. Drain; wipe drippings from pan with paper towels.

Return turkey mixture to Dutch oven. Add tomato and next 6 ingredients. Bring to a boil over medium-high heat. Reduce heat to low; cover and simmer 30 minutes. Transfer turkey mixture to a shallow 2½-quart casserole coated with cooking spray. Drop Cornbread Dumplings batter by tablespoons onto chili, leaving space between batter. Bake at 425° for 20 minutes or until dumplings are browned. Yield: 6 servings.

CORNBREAD DUMPLINGS
½ cup yellow cornmeal
¼ cup plus 2 tablespoons all-purpose flour
1 teaspoon baking powder
1 teaspoon chili powder
½ teaspoon sugar
¼ teaspoon salt
⅓ cup skim milk
2 tablespoons frozen egg substitute, thawed
1½ tablespoons reduced-calorie margarine,
    melted
¼ cup (1 ounce) shredded 40% less-fat
    Cheddar cheese
1½ tablespoons minced green onions

Combine first 6 ingredients in a medium bowl; make a well in the center of cornmeal mixture. Combine milk, egg substitute, and margarine in a small bowl; add to dry ingredients, stirring just until dry ingredients are moistened. Gently stir in cheese and green onions. Yield: 6 servings.

PER SERVING: 382 CALORIES (19% FROM FAT)
FAT 8.0G (SATURATED FAT 2.2G)
PROTEIN 35.0G   CARBOHYDRATE 42.2G
CHOLESTEROL 67MG   SODIUM 658MG

TURKEY-WILD RICE CASSEROLE

3 cups canned low-sodium chicken broth,
    undiluted
3 cups sliced fresh mushrooms
1 cup (6 ounces) wild rice, uncooked
3 cups chopped cooked turkey breast
⅔ cup commercial oil-free Italian dressing
1 cup low-fat sour cream
Vegetable cooking spray

Bring chicken broth to a boil in a medium saucepan; stir in mushrooms. Reduce heat; simmer 5 minutes. Remove mushrooms with a slotted spoon. Add rice to pan; stir well. Cover and cook 1 hour and 5 minutes or until liquid is absorbed and rice is tender.

Combine rice, mushrooms, turkey, dressing, and sour cream; spoon into a 2-quart baking dish coated with cooking spray. Bake, uncovered, at 325° for 45 minutes. Let stand 10 minutes before serving. Yield: 6 servings.

PER SERVING: 298 CALORIES (20% FROM FAT)
FAT 6.7G (SATURATED FAT 4.0G)
PROTEIN 30.6G   CARBOHYDRATE 28.6G
CHOLESTEROL 80MG   SODIUM 382MG

Cornish Hens with Fruited Wild Rice

CORNISH HENS WITH FRUITED WILD RICE

¼ cup chopped dried figs
¼ cup chopped dried apricots
2 tablespoons apricot brandy or nectar
¼ cup canned low-sodium chicken broth, undiluted
½ cup chopped fresh mushrooms
¼ cup minced shallots
1⅓ cups cooked wild rice (cooked without salt or fat)
¼ cup chopped extra-lean cured cooked ham
3 tablespoons chopped walnuts, toasted
2 (1-pound) Cornish hens, skinned
1 teaspoon olive oil
1 teaspoon paprika
1 teaspoon pepper
Apricot wedges (optional)
Fresh thyme (optional)

Combine figs and apricots in a small bowl. Bring brandy to a simmer in a small saucepan; pour over fig mixture. Cover and let stand 15 minutes.

Bring chicken broth to a boil in a small skillet over medium-high heat. Add mushrooms and shallots; sauté 5 minutes or until vegetables are tender and liquid has evaporated.

Cut 4 (18- x 15-inch) rectangles of parchment paper; fold each rectangle in half lengthwise, and trim each into a heart shape. Place parchment hearts on 2 large baking sheets, and open out flat. Combine fig mixture, mushroom mixture, rice, ham, and walnuts; stir well. Spoon one-fourth of rice mixture on one side of each parchment heart near the crease.

Remove giblets from hens; reserve for another use. Rinse hens under cold water, and pat dry. Split each hen in half lengthwise, using an electric knife. Place hen halves, cut side down, on rice mixture. Rub hens with olive oil; sprinkle with paprika and pepper.

Fold parchment paper edges over to seal. Starting with rounded edges, pleat and crimp edges together to seal. Bake at 325° for 40 minutes or until hens are done.

Transfer hens and rice mixture to serving plates. If desired, garnish with apricot wedges and thyme. Yield: 4 servings.

PER SERVING: 324 CALORIES (24% FROM FAT)
FAT 8.6G (SATURATED FAT 1.4G)
PROTEIN 30.2G   CARBOHYDRATE 32.9G
CHOLESTEROL 81MG   SODIUM 208MG

BAKED SEA BASS AND VEGETABLES

Vegetable cooking spray
2 tablespoons reduced-calorie margarine
3 cups finely chopped round red potato
1 cup chopped onion
¾ cup chopped carrot
2 teaspoons minced garlic
2 cups thinly sliced sweet red pepper
2 cups peeled, seeded, and chopped tomato
1 cup canned low-sodium chicken broth, undiluted
3 tablespoons sliced ripe olives
2 teaspoons capers, drained
½ teaspoon dried thyme
6 (4-ounce) sea bass fillets (1 inch thick)
2 tablespoons fresh lemon juice

Coat a large nonstick skillet with cooking spray; add margarine. Place over medium heat until margarine melts. Add potato, onion, carrot, and garlic; cover and cook 3 minutes. Add pepper and next 5 ingredients; cover and cook an additional 15 minutes or until vegetables are crisp-tender.

Place fillets over vegetable mixture; cover and cook 10 minutes or until fish flakes easily when tested with a fork. Transfer fillets and vegetable mixture to a serving platter, using a slotted spoon. Drizzle lemon juice evenly over fillets and vegetable mixture. Yield: 6 servings.

PER SERVING: 258 CALORIES (23% FROM FAT)
FAT 6.5G (SATURATED FAT 0.8G)
PROTEIN 24.3G   CARBOHYDRATE 26.7G
CHOLESTEROL 47MG   SODIUM 287MG

SHRIMP AND RICE BAKE

1½ pounds medium-size fresh shrimp, cooked,
   peeled, and deveined
Vegetable cooking spray
2 cups sliced fresh mushrooms
½ cup chopped onion
½ cup chopped green onions
3 cups cooked long-grain rice (cooked without
   salt or fat)
¾ cup low-fat sour cream
2 tablespoons reduced-calorie mayonnaise
2 teaspoons prepared mustard
1 cup (4 ounces) shredded 40% less-fat
   Cheddar cheese
1 tablespoon chopped fresh parsley

Cut shrimp in half lengthwise. Set aside. Coat a
nonstick skillet with cooking spray; place over
medium-high heat until hot. Add mushrooms, onion,
and green onions; sauté until tender. Set aside.

Place cooked rice in a 2-quart baking dish coated
with cooking spray; arrange shrimp over rice.

Combine sour cream, mayonnaise, and mustard
in a small bowl; spoon sour cream mixture over
shrimp. Top with reserved mushroom mixture.
Sprinkle cheese over top. Cover; bake at 350° for
30 minutes or until thoroughly heated. Top with
chopped parsley. Yield: 6 servings.

PER SERVING: 297 CALORIES (28% FROM FAT)
FAT 9.3G (SATURATED FAT 4.3G)
PROTEIN 20.8G   CARBOHYDRATE 33.3G
CHOLESTEROL 125MG   SODIUM 304MG

FYI

Cleaning an oven is no fun. To prevent
spillovers, use the recommended containers
for baking. Containers that are too small can
cause food to bubble over. But pans that are
too large can cause food to dry out.

SPINACH AND MUSHROOM QUICHE

¾ cup all-purpose flour
¼ teaspoon salt
2 tablespoons vegetable oil
2 tablespoons cold water
Vegetable cooking spray
2 cups sliced fresh mushrooms
½ cup chopped onion
2 cloves garlic, minced
1 cup nonfat cottage cheese
¾ cup frozen egg substitute, thawed
½ cup skim milk
1 tablespoon Dijon mustard
¼ teaspoon pepper
¼ teaspoon ground thyme
1 (10-ounce) package frozen chopped spinach,
   thawed and drained
¼ cup plus 2 tablespoons (1½ ounces)
   shredded reduced-fat Swiss cheese

Combine flour and salt. Combine oil and water;
stir well. Add oil mixture to dry ingredients, stirring
with a fork just until dry ingredients are moistened.
Shape into a ball; chill 30 minutes.

Roll dough to ⅛-inch thickness between 2 sheets
of heavy-duty plastic wrap. Place in freezer 5 minutes. Remove bottom sheet of plastic wrap. Fit
dough into a 10-inch quiche dish; remove top sheet
of plastic wrap. Fold edges of dough under and
flute, if desired. Prick bottom of pastry shell lightly
with a fork. Bake at 400° for 15 minutes or until
golden.

Coat a nonstick skillet with cooking spray; place
over medium-high heat until hot. Add mushrooms,
onion, and garlic; sauté until tender. Combine cottage cheese and next 5 ingredients; stir in spinach
and mushroom mixture. Spoon mixture into prepared pastry shell. Bake at 350° for 35 minutes.
Remove from oven, and sprinkle with Swiss
cheese. Bake 5 minutes or until cheese melts. Let
stand 10 minutes before slicing. Yield: 6 servings.

PER SERVING: 194 CALORIES (30% FROM FAT)
FAT 6.5G (SATURATED FAT 1.6G)
PROTEIN 15.0G   CARBOHYDRATE 19.7G
CHOLESTEROL 6MG   SODIUM 415MG

PESTO-STUFFED SHELLS

(pictured on page 100)

Vegetable cooking spray
1¾ cups finely chopped sweet red pepper
   (about 2 medium)
½ cup chopped onion
2 cloves garlic, minced
1 (14½-ounce) can no-salt-added whole
   tomatoes, undrained
1 (8-ounce) can no-salt-added tomato sauce
½ teaspoon dried Italian seasoning
¼ teaspoon salt
¼ teaspoon ground white pepper
12 jumbo pasta shells (4½ ounces), uncooked
½ pound firm tofu
1¼ cups part-skim ricotta cheese
¼ cup grated Parmesan cheese
½ cup minced fresh basil
½ cup minced fresh parsley

Coat a large nonstick skillet with cooking spray; place over medium-high heat until hot. Add sweet red pepper, onion, and garlic; sauté until tender.

Place sautéed vegetables and tomatoes in container of an electric blender or food processor; cover; process until smooth. Pour into a medium saucepan. Add tomato sauce, Italian seasoning, salt, and white pepper; stir well. Bring to a boil; reduce heat, and simmer, uncovered, 20 minutes. Spread ½ cup tomato sauce mixture into an 11- x 7- x 2-inch baking dish coated with cooking spray; set aside. Reserve remaining tomato sauce mixture.

Cook pasta shells according to package directions, omitting salt and fat; drain and set aside.

Wrap tofu in several layers of cheesecloth or paper towels; press lightly to remove excess moisture. Remove cheesecloth; crumble tofu.

Position knife blade in food processor bowl; add tofu and remaining ingredients. Process 1 minute or until smooth. Spoon tofu mixture into pasta shells; place filled shells in prepared baking dish. Top with remaining tomato sauce mixture. Cover; bake at 400° for 40 minutes. Yield: 4 servings.

PER SERVING: 349 CALORIES (28% FROM FAT)
FAT 10.7G (SATURATED FAT 4.9G)
PROTEIN 20.8G   CARBOHYDRATE 43.4G
CHOLESTEROL 26MG   SODIUM 369MG

BAKED POTATOES WITH BROCCOLI AND CHEESE

6 (8-ounce) baking potatoes
½ cup plain nonfat yogurt
3 tablespoons minced onion
¼ teaspoon salt
⅛ teaspoon ground white pepper
5 cups chopped fresh broccoli (about 1¾
   pounds)
2 teaspoons reduced-calorie margarine
2 tablespoons cornstarch
1 tablespoon plus 1 teaspoon water
⅔ cup canned low-sodium chicken broth,
   undiluted
⅔ cup skim milk
¾ cup (3 ounces) shredded reduced-fat mild
   Cheddar cheese
Paprika

Scrub potatoes; bake at 400° for 1 hour or until soft. Let cool to touch. Cut a lengthwise strip (1 inch wide) from top of each potato; carefully scoop out pulp, leaving shells intact.

Combine potato pulp, yogurt, and next 3 ingredients in a large bowl. Beat at medium speed of an electric mixer until light and fluffy; spoon mixture evenly into shells. Bake at 400° for 25 to 30 minutes or until thoroughly heated.

Arrange broccoli in a vegetable steamer over boiling water. Cover and steam 8 minutes or until crisp-tender. Set aside.

Melt margarine in a heavy saucepan over medium heat. Combine cornstarch and water, stirring well; add to margarine, stirring until smooth. Cook 1 minute, stirring constantly. Gradually add chicken broth and milk; cook over medium heat, stirring constantly, until thickened. Add cheese, stirring until cheese melts. Stir in broccoli; cook just until thoroughly heated.

Spoon broccoli-cheese mixture evenly over potatoes. Sprinkle with paprika. Yield: 6 servings.

PER SERVING: 352 CALORIES (10% FROM FAT)
FAT 4.1G (SATURATED FAT 1.8G)
PROTEIN 13.5G   CARBOHYDRATE 67.2G
CHOLESTEROL 10MG   SODIUM 282MG

Vegetarian Couscous Casserole

VEGETARIAN COUSCOUS CASSEROLE

1½ cups water
¼ teaspoon salt
1 cup couscous, uncooked
1 (15-ounce) can black beans, drained
1 (8¾-ounce) can no-salt-added whole kernel
　corn, drained
1 (8-ounce) can sliced water chestnuts,
　drained
1 (7-ounce) jar roasted red peppers in water,
　drained and cut into strips
⅓ cup minced green onions
2 tablespoons minced pickled jalapeño pepper
1 cup part-skim ricotta cheese
2 tablespoons balsamic vinegar
2 teaspoons sesame oil
1 teaspoon ground cumin
Vegetable cooking spray
Chopped green onions (optional)
6 cups fresh spinach leaves

Combine water and salt in a saucepan; bring to a boil. Remove from heat. Add couscous; stir well. Cover and let stand 5 minutes or until couscous is tender and liquid is absorbed. Add black beans and next 5 ingredients; stir gently.

Combine ricotta cheese, vinegar, oil, and cumin; stir into couscous mixture. Spoon mixture into an 11- x 7- x 2-inch baking dish coated with cooking spray. Bake, uncovered, at 350° for 25 minutes or until thoroughly heated. Sprinkle with chopped green onions, if desired.

Cut spinach leaves into thin strips. Place 1 cup spinach on each serving plate; spoon couscous mixture evenly over spinach. Yield: 6 servings.

PER SERVING: 291 CALORIES (19% FROM FAT)
FAT 6.1G (SATURATED FAT 2.3G)
PROTEIN 15.2G　CARBOHYDRATE 46.0G
CHOLESTEROL 13MG　SODIUM 208MG

ITALIAN ROTINI CASSEROLE

Vegetable cooking spray
1½ cups diced zucchini
½ cup chopped fresh mushrooms
¼ cup chopped onion
1½ tablespoons reduced-calorie margarine
1 tablespoon all-purpose flour
1¼ cups no-salt-added tomato juice
½ teaspoon dried basil
½ teaspoon dried oregano
¼ teaspoon salt
3 cups cooked tri-color rotini (corkscrew pasta), cooked without salt or fat
1 (16-ounce) can light red kidney beans, drained
1½ cups (6 ounces) shredded part-skim mozzarella cheese
1½ tablespoons grated Parmesan cheese

Coat a small nonstick skillet with cooking spray; place over medium-high heat until hot. Add zucchini, mushrooms, and onion; sauté until tender. Remove from heat, and set aside.

Melt margarine in a small, heavy saucepan over medium heat; add flour, stirring until smooth. Cook 1 minute, stirring constantly. Gradually add tomato juice; cook, stirring constantly, until mixture is thickened and bubbly. Remove from heat, and stir in basil, oregano, and salt.

Combine sauce mixture, vegetable mixture, pasta, beans, and mozzarella cheese; stir well. Pour mixture into a 2-quart casserole coated with cooking spray. Sprinkle evenly with Parmesan cheese. Cover and bake at 350° for 20 minutes; uncover and bake an additional 10 minutes or until thoroughly heated. Yield: 6 servings.

PER SERVING: 294 CALORIES (24% FROM FAT)
FAT 7.7G (SATURATED FAT 3.5G)
PROTEIN 16.8G   CARBOHYDRATE 40.3G
CHOLESTEROL 17MG   SODIUM 287MG

LENTIL PASTICCIO

This Grecian-inspired casserole is kept low in fat by calling for skim milk instead of whole in the white sauce.

1 cup elbow macaroni, uncooked
¾ cup dried lentils
¾ cup chopped onion
1 medium carrot, finely chopped
1 clove garlic, minced
1¾ cups water
1 (8-ounce) can no-salt-added tomato sauce
2 tablespoons chopped fresh parsley
¼ teaspoon ground cinnamon
1 tablespoon margarine
1½ tablespoons all-purpose flour
1 cup skim milk
¼ cup grated Parmesan cheese
¼ teaspoon salt
⅛ teaspoon pepper
¼ cup frozen egg substitute, thawed
Vegetable cooking spray

Cook macaroni according to package directions, omitting salt and fat; drain well, and set aside.

Combine lentils, onion, carrot, garlic, and water in a medium saucepan. Bring to a boil; cover, reduce heat, and simmer 35 minutes. (Do not overcook lentils.) Remove from heat; stir in tomato sauce, parsley, and cinnamon. Set aside.

Melt margarine in a medium saucepan over medium heat; add flour, stirring until smooth. Cook 1 minute, stirring constantly. Gradually add milk; cook, stirring constantly, until thickened and bubbly. Remove from heat. Add Parmesan cheese, salt, and pepper, stirring until cheese melts. Let cool; stir in egg substitute.

Layer half each of macaroni and lentil mixture in a 10- x 6- x 2-inch baking dish coated with cooking spray. Repeat layers; pour cheese mixture evenly over top. Bake, uncovered, at 350° for 45 minutes or until lightly browned. Let stand 10 minutes. Yield: 6 servings.

PER SERVING: 240 CALORIES (14% FROM FAT)
FAT 3.7G (SATURATED FAT 1.2G)
PROTEIN 14.1G   CARBOHYDRATE 38.3G
CHOLESTEROL 3MG   SODIUM 235MG

INTERNATIONAL FLAVORS

*M*exicans enjoy enchiladas, and the Japanese eat sukiyaki. French families make a meal of cassoulet, and children in Spain grow up on paella. But what is everyday one-dish fare in another part of the world can create a sensation at your table.

Many of these international classics, such as Beef Burgundy (page 135), contain a regional starchy food (often pasta, rice, or tortillas), meat, and vegetables all under one lid. To round out a menu, consider a fruit side dish with the Mexican dishes, crusty bread with those from Italy, and a green salad for recipes of French origin.

Vegetarian Tacos (Recipe follows on page 127)

CHICKEN TOSTADAS WITH RED PEPPER SALSA

Vegetable cooking spray
6 (4-ounce) skinned, boned chicken breast
   halves, cubed
1½ cups chopped onion
2 cloves garlic, minced
Red Pepper Salsa, divided
¼ cup Chablis or other dry white wine
½ teaspoon chili powder
¼ teaspoon salt
⅛ teaspoon freshly ground pepper
8 (6-inch) corn tortillas
2 cups shredded lettuce
½ cup nonfat sour cream alternative

Coat a large nonstick skillet with cooking spray; place over medium-high heat until hot. Add chicken, onion, and garlic; cook until chicken is browned. Drain chicken, and pat dry with paper towels. Wipe drippings from skillet with a paper towel.

Add chicken mixture, ¾ cup Red Pepper Salsa, and next 4 ingredients to skillet. Bring to a boil; cover, reduce heat, and simmer 10 minutes. Uncover and increase heat to high. Cook 5 minutes or until liquid has evaporated.

Place tortillas on ungreased baking sheets. Bake at 350° for 15 minutes or until crisp. Place 1 tortilla on each of 8 serving plates. Top each evenly with lettuce, chicken mixture, remaining 2 cups Red Pepper Salsa, and sour cream. Yield: 8 servings.

RED PEPPER SALSA

2 medium-size sweet red peppers, roasted and
   peeled
1 Anaheim chile, roasted and peeled
1½ cups peeled, seeded, and chopped tomato
2 jalapeño peppers, seeded and chopped
1 clove garlic, minced
2 teaspoons red wine vinegar
½ teaspoon ground cumin
¼ teaspoon salt

Chicken Tostadas with Red Pepper Salsa

Chop peppers and chile; place in a bowl. Stir in remaining ingredients. Cover and chill thoroughly. Yield: 2¾ cups.

PER SERVING: 199 CALORIES (17% FROM FAT)
FAT 3.8G (SATURATED FAT 0.9G)
PROTEIN 23.1G   CARBOHYDRATE 17.8G
CHOLESTEROL 54MG   SODIUM 245MG

Directions for Roasting Peppers: Cut peppers in half lengthwise; remove and discard seeds and membrane. Place peppers, skin side up, on a baking sheet; flatten with palm of hand. Broil 5½ inches from heat (with electric door partially opened) 15 to 20 minutes or until peppers are charred. Place in ice water, and chill 5 minutes. Remove peppers from water; peel and discard skins.

TURKEY BURRITOS

Vegetable cooking spray
1 pound freshly ground raw turkey
½ cup commercial medium-hot taco sauce
1½ cups diced unpeeled tomato
1¼ cups diced unpeeled zucchini
½ cup diced onion
½ cup diced green pepper
¼ teaspoon salt
¼ teaspoon pepper
8 (8-inch) flour tortillas
½ cup (2 ounces) shredded reduced-fat
   Cheddar cheese

Coat a nonstick skillet with cooking spray; place over medium heat. Add turkey; cook until browned and crumbly. Drain; pat dry with paper towels. Wipe drippings from skillet. Combine turkey and taco sauce; stir well. Set aside; keep warm.

Add tomato and next 3 ingredients to skillet; sauté 5 minutes or until crisp-tender. Drain. Stir in salt and pepper.

Spoon turkey and vegetables down center of 8 tortillas. Top with cheese; roll up. Yield: 8 servings.

PER SERVING: 276 CALORIES (22% FROM FAT)
FAT 6.8G (SATURATED FAT 2.0G)
PROTEIN 19.1G   CARBOHYDRATE 33.4G
CHOLESTEROL 37MG   SODIUM 454MG

BEEF AND SALSA FAJITAS

¼ cup lime juice
¼ cup light beer
2 tablespoons minced fresh cilantro
1 teaspoon dried oregano
¼ teaspoon ground red pepper
2 cloves garlic, minced
1 small green pepper
1 small sweet red pepper
1 small sweet yellow pepper
1 (1-pound) lean boneless top round steak
1 small purple onion, cut into 8 wedges
1 cup diced tomato
2 tablespoons chopped green onions
2 tablespoons minced fresh cilantro
2 tablespoons red wine vinegar
1 tablespoon chopped ripe olives
1 tablespoon seeded, minced jalapeño pepper
Vegetable cooking spray
8 (8-inch) flour tortillas

Combine first 6 ingredients in a heavy-duty, zip-top plastic bag; seal bag and shake. Seed green and sweet peppers; cut each into 8 wedges. Place pepper wedges, steak, and onion in bag; seal bag and shake. Marinate in refrigerator 8 hours. Combine tomato and next 5 ingredients. Cover and chill.

Remove steak and vegetables from marinade, reserving marinade. Thread vegetables onto 4 (10-inch) metal skewers. Coat grill rack with cooking spray; place on grill over medium-hot coals (350° to 400°). Place steak and skewers on rack. Grill vegetables, covered, 12 minutes or until tender, turning and basting occasionally. Grill steak 5 to 6 minutes on each side or to desired degree of doneness, basting occasionally. Wrap tortillas in aluminum foil. Grill, covered, 2 minutes.

Cut steak diagonally across grain into ¼-inch-wide slices. Divide steak and vegetables among tortillas. Top each with 3 tablespoons tomato salsa mixture; roll up tortillas. Yield: 8 servings.

PER SERVING: 234 CALORIES (23% FROM FAT)
FAT 5.9G (SATURATED FAT 1.4G)
PROTEIN 18.2G   CARBOHYDRATE 26.6G
CHOLESTEROL 37MG   SODIUM 212MG

BAKED PORK CHIMICHANGAS

2 pounds lean boneless pork
2 cups water
2 tablespoons chili powder
2 tablespoons white vinegar
½ teaspoon dried oregano
½ teaspoon ground cumin
2 cloves garlic, minced
1 (8-ounce) can no-salt-added tomato sauce
1 (4-ounce) can chopped green chiles
1 cup (4 ounces) shredded reduced-fat
   Monterey Jack cheese
½ cup sliced green onions
12 (10-inch) flour tortillas
Vegetable cooking spray
12 cups shredded iceberg lettuce
¾ cup nonfat sour cream alternative
¼ teaspoon hot sauce
¾ cup commercial no-salt-added salsa

Trim fat from pork; cut pork into 2-inch pieces. Combine pork, water, and next 5 ingredients in a saucepan; bring to a boil. Cover, reduce heat, and simmer 30 minutes. Uncover; cook over medium-low heat 1 hour or until liquid evaporates. Remove from heat; shred meat with 2 forks. Stir in tomato sauce, chiles, cheese, and green onions.

Wrap tortillas in aluminum foil; heat at 350° for 15 minutes. Working with 1 tortilla at a time, coat both sides with cooking spray. Spoon about ⅓ cup meat mixture just below center of tortilla. Fold over left and right sides of tortilla to partially enclose filling. Fold remaining edges to form a rectangle, and secure with a wooden pick. Repeat procedure with remaining tortillas and meat mixture.

Place filled tortillas on an ungreased baking sheet. Bake at 425° for 20 minutes or until crisp. Remove wooden picks. Place 1 cup lettuce on each of 12 plates; top with chimichangas. Combine sour cream and hot sauce. Top each chimichanga with sour cream mixture and salsa. Yield: 12 servings.

PER SERVING: 367 CALORIES (30% FROM FAT)
FAT 12.2G (SATURATED FAT 3.7G)
PROTEIN 25.7G   CARBOHYDRATE 37.4G
CHOLESTEROL 52MG   SODIUM 423MG

SPICY PINTO BEAN BURRITOS

6 (9-inch) flour tortillas
Vegetable cooking spray
1 teaspoon olive oil
½ cup chopped onion
1 jalapeño pepper, seeded and minced
1 teaspoon minced garlic
2 cups canned pinto beans, drained, rinsed,
   and mashed
½ cup nonfat process cream cheese product,
   softened
¼ cup nonfat mayonnaise
½ cup chopped green onions
¼ cup plus 2 tablespoons no-salt-added salsa
½ cup (2 ounces) shredded reduced-fat
   Cheddar cheese
3 cups finely shredded lettuce
1 cup seeded, chopped tomato
½ cup chopped green pepper
2 tablespoons chopped fresh cilantro

Place a damp paper towel in center of a sheet of aluminum foil. Stack tortillas on paper towel. Cover stack with another damp paper towel; seal foil. Bake at 250° for 10 minutes.

Coat a nonstick skillet with cooking spray; add olive oil. Place over medium heat until hot. Add ½ cup onion; sauté 4 minutes. Add jalapeño and garlic; sauté 1 minute. Add pinto beans; cook 3 minutes or until thoroughly heated, stirring frequently. Combine cream cheese and mayonnaise; stir well.

Spoon about ¼ cup bean mixture down one side of each tortilla. Top evenly with cream cheese mixture, green onions, and salsa. Roll up tortillas; arrange seam side down in a 13- x 9- x 2-inch baking dish coated with cooking spray. Cover and bake at 350° for 20 minutes. Sprinkle with Cheddar cheese; bake, uncovered, 5 minutes or until cheese melts. Place ½ cup lettuce and 1 burrito on each plate. Top burritos evenly with tomato, green pepper, and cilantro. Yield: 6 servings.

PER SERVING: 345 CALORIES (19% FROM FAT)
FAT 7.2G (SATURATED FAT 1.9G)
PROTEIN 16.3G   CARBOHYDRATE 53.7G
CHOLESTEROL 10MG   SODIUM 789MG

VEGETABLE ENCHILADA CASSEROLE

Vegetable cooking spray
¾ cup chopped green pepper
½ cup chopped green onions
2 cloves garlic, minced
1 small eggplant, peeled and chopped
1 medium zucchini, sliced
½ pound fresh mushrooms, sliced
1 (8-ounce) can no-salt-added tomato sauce
1 (8-ounce) can chopped green chiles, drained
1 cup chopped tomato
1 teaspoon sugar
½ teaspoon chili powder
⅛ teaspoon ground cumin
6 (8-inch) flour tortillas
½ cup (2 ounces) shredded reduced-fat mild
   Cheddar cheese
½ cup (2 ounces) shredded reduced-fat
   Monterey Jack cheese
¼ cup sliced ripe olives

Coat a large nonstick skillet with cooking spray; place over medium-high heat until hot. Add green pepper, green onions, and garlic; sauté until crisp-tender. Add eggplant, zucchini, and mushrooms; sauté 4 to 5 minutes or until vegetables are tender, stirring occasionally. Stir in tomato sauce and next 5 ingredients; cover and simmer 30 minutes, stirring occasionally.

Coat a 13- x 9- x 2-inch baking dish with cooking spray. Arrange half of tortillas in dish; top with vegetable mixture. Arrange remaining half of tortillas over vegetable mixture. Cover and bake at 350° for 25 to 30 minutes or until thoroughly heated. Sprinkle with shredded cheeses and olives; bake, uncovered, an additional 5 minutes or until cheese melts. Yield: 6 servings.

PER SERVING: 261 CALORIES (27% FROM FAT)
FAT 7.7G (SATURATED FAT 2.7G)
PROTEIN 12.1G   CARBOHYDRATE 37.6G
CHOLESTEROL 12MG   SODIUM 401MG

VEGETARIAN TACOS
(pictured on page 122)

1½ cups shredded zucchini
1½ cups shredded yellow squash
1 cup cored, seeded, and chopped sweet red
   pepper
½ cup chopped onion
¼ cup red wine vinegar
1 teaspoon vegetable oil
½ teaspoon ground cumin
¼ teaspoon salt
⅛ teaspoon pepper
1½ cups canned black beans, rinsed and
   drained
1 cup canned navy beans, rinsed and drained
¼ cup water
½ teaspoon chili powder
¼ teaspoon garlic powder
¼ teaspoon dried crushed red pepper
¼ teaspoon salt
8 (6-inch) flour tortillas
½ cup (2 ounces) shredded Monterey Jack
   cheese with jalapeño peppers
½ cup (2 ounces) shredded 40% less-fat
   Cheddar cheese
Fresh cilantro sprigs (optional)

Combine first 4 ingredients in a medium bowl; set aside. Combine vinegar, oil, cumin, ¼ teaspoon salt, and pepper; stir well. Pour over vegetable mixture; toss well. Set aside.

Place beans, water, chili powder, garlic powder, crushed red pepper, and ¼ teaspoon salt in a medium saucepan. Bring mixture to a boil over medium heat. Reduce heat, and simmer, uncovered, 3 to 5 minutes or until beans are thoroughly heated and most of liquid has evaporated.

Wrap tortillas in aluminum foil; bake at 350° for 10 minutes. Spoon vegetable mixture evenly down center of each tortilla, using a slotted spoon. Top each with bean mixture; sprinkle with cheeses. Roll tortillas; secure with wooden picks. Garnish with cilantro sprigs, if desired. Yield: 8 servings.

PER SERVING: 267 CALORIES (24% FROM FAT)
FAT 7.1G (SATURATED FAT 2.7G)
PROTEIN 13.2G   CARBOHYDRATE 38.3G
CHOLESTEROL 10MG   SODIUM 598MG

Vegetable Quesadillas

VEGETABLE QUESADILLAS

1 cup frozen black-eyed peas
1 cup water, divided
1 cup seeded, diced tomato
¼ cup peeled, diced avocado
2½ tablespoons minced fresh cilantro
2 tablespoons minced purple onion
1 tablespoon seeded, minced jalapeño pepper
2 tablespoons fresh lime juice
¼ teaspoon ground cumin
⅛ teaspoon garlic powder
Vegetable cooking spray
1 cup julienne-sliced zucchini
1 cup frozen whole kernel corn, thawed
4 (8-inch) flour tortillas
¾ cup (3 ounces) shredded reduced-fat
    Cheddar cheese
¾ cup (3 ounces) shredded reduced-fat
    Monterey Jack cheese
Fresh cilantro sprigs (optional)

Combine peas and ½ cup water in a small saucepan; bring to a boil. Cover, reduce heat, and simmer 35 to 40 minutes or until tender; drain well.

Combine remaining ½ cup water, tomato, and next 7 ingredients in a medium bowl; stir well.

Coat a large nonstick skillet with cooking spray; place over medium-high heat until hot. Add zucchini; sauté 3 minutes or until tender. Add corn; sauté 2 minutes. Remove from heat; stir in peas.

Place 2 tortillas on a baking sheet coated with cooking spray; top tortillas with cheeses and zucchini mixture. Top with remaining tortillas. Bake at 400° for 8 minutes or just until tortillas are crisp and cheese melts. Cut each in half. Place on individual plates; top with tomato mixture. Garnish with cilantro, if desired. Yield: 4 servings.

PER SERVING: 392 CALORIES (31% FROM FAT)
FAT 13.3G (SATURATED FAT 5.6G)
PROTEIN 22.5G   CARBOHYDRATE 49.1G
CHOLESTEROL 28MG   SODIUM 474MG

MUSHROOM-SPINACH CALZONES

1 package dry yeast
1 cup warm water (105° to 115°), divided
1 tablespoon honey
½ teaspoon salt
1¾ cups whole wheat flour
1 cup unbleached flour
3 tablespoons whole wheat flour, divided
Vegetable cooking spray
1½ cups sliced fresh mushrooms
1½ cups tightly packed chopped fresh spinach
¾ cup chopped onion
¾ cup diced sweet red pepper
½ cup shredded carrot
¼ cup commercial oil-free Italian dressing
1½ cups (6 ounces) shredded part-skim
    mozzarella cheese
¼ teaspoon freshly ground pepper
1 egg white
1 tablespoon water

Dissolve yeast in ¼ cup warm water in a large bowl; let stand 5 minutes. Combine remaining ¾ cup warm water, honey, and salt; add to yeast mixture, stirring gently. Gradually stir in 1¾ cups whole wheat flour and enough unbleached flour to make a soft dough.

Sprinkle 1 tablespoon whole wheat flour evenly over work surface. Turn dough out onto surface, and knead until smooth and elastic (about 8 to 10 minutes). Place dough in a large bowl coated with cooking spray, turning to coat top. Cover and let rise in a warm place (85°), free from drafts, 45 minutes or until doubled in bulk.

Coat a nonstick skillet with cooking spray; place over medium-high heat until hot. Add mushrooms and next 4 ingredients; sauté until crisp-tender. Remove from heat; stir in dressing. Set aside.

Punch dough down, and divide into 6 portions. Shape each into a ball; cover and let rest 5 minutes. Sprinkle 1 teaspoon flour evenly over work surface. Turn 1 portion of dough out onto floured surface; roll into a 7½-inch circle. Repeat procedure with remaining flour and portions of dough.

Spoon vegetable mixture evenly over half of each circle. Sprinkle cheese and ground pepper over each. Brush edges of circles with water. Fold circles in half; crimp edges to seal. Combine egg white and 1 tablespoon water; brush calzones. Place on ungreased baking sheet. Bake at 425° for 10 minutes or until golden. Yield: 6 servings.

PER SERVING: 318 CALORIES (17% FROM FAT)
FAT 5.9G (SATURATED FAT 3.1G)
PROTEIN 16.5G CARBOHYDRATE 52.8G
CHOLESTEROL 16MG SODIUM 460MG

SPICY TURKEY CHILI

Vegetable cooking spray
2 pounds freshly ground raw turkey
1½ cups chopped onion
1 clove garlic, minced
2½ cups water
2 tablespoons chili powder
1 tablespoon dried parsley flakes
1 teaspoon paprika
1 teaspoon dry mustard
⅛ teaspoon salt
2 (16-ounce) cans red kidney beans, drained
2 (4-ounce) cans mushroom stems and pieces, drained
1 (14½-ounce) can no-salt-added stewed tomatoes, undrained
1 (10-ounce) can diced tomatoes and green chiles, undrained
1 bay leaf

Coat a Dutch oven with cooking spray; place over medium-high heat until hot. Add turkey, onion, and garlic, and cook 9 minutes or until turkey is browned, stirring until it crumbles. Drain and wipe drippings from pan with a paper towel.

Return mixture to pan. Add water and remaining ingredients; bring to a boil. Cover, reduce heat, and simmer 1 hour. Uncover; simmer 1 hour, stirring occasionally. Discard bay leaf. Yield: 7 (1½-cup) servings.

PER SERVING: 320 CALORIES (16% FROM FAT)
FAT 5.8G (SATURATED FAT 1.7G)
PROTEIN 37.3G CARBOHYDRATE 28.5G
CHOLESTEROL 74MG SODIUM 579MG

VEGETABLE LASAGNA

Vegetable cooking spray
1 cup chopped onion
½ cup chopped green pepper
2 cloves garlic, minced
1½ cups peeled, chopped tomato
1½ cups sliced fresh mushrooms
2 cups no-salt-added tomato sauce
1 cup shredded carrot
¼ cup no-salt-added beef broth, undiluted
1 (6-ounce) can no-salt-added tomato paste
2½ tablespoons chopped fresh basil
1 tablespoon chopped fresh oregano
½ teaspoon dried Italian seasoning
½ teaspoon pepper
1 (10-ounce) package frozen chopped spinach,
    thawed
1 (15-ounce) carton lite ricotta cheese
½ cup nonfat cottage cheese
1 cup (4 ounces) shredded part-skim
    mozzarella cheese, divided
9 cooked lasagna noodles (cooked without salt
    or fat)
2 tablespoons grated Parmesan cheese

Coat a Dutch oven with cooking spray; place over medium heat until hot. Add onion, green pepper, and garlic; sauté until tender. Add tomato and next 9 ingredients. Bring to a boil. Cover, reduce heat, and simmer 20 minutes. Add spinach; simmer 5 minutes.

Position blade in food processor; add ricotta and cottage cheeses. Process until blended. Stir in ½ cup mozzarella cheese. Spoon 1 cup vegetable mixture into a 13- x 9- x 2-inch baking dish coated with cooking spray. Layer with 3 noodles, one-third of remaining vegetable mixture, and half of cheese mixture. Repeat layers once. Top with remaining noodles and vegetable mixture. Cover and bake at 350° for 25 minutes. Uncover and sprinkle with remaining ½ cup mozzarella cheese and Parmesan cheese. Bake 10 minutes. Yield: 8 servings.

PER SERVING: 256 CALORIES (19% FROM FAT)
FAT 5.4G (SATURATED FAT 2.9G)
PROTEIN 18.4G   CARBOHYDRATE 37.5G
CHOLESTEROL 17MG   SODIUM 245MG

ZUCCHINI-BEEF SPAGHETTI

Vegetable cooking spray
1 pound ultra-lean ground beef
2 cups sliced fresh mushrooms
2 cups thinly sliced zucchini
1 cup chopped onion
½ teaspoon salt
¼ teaspoon crushed red pepper
4 cloves garlic, minced
1 (14½-ounce) can no-salt-added whole
    tomatoes, undrained and chopped
1 cup water
1 (6-ounce) can no-salt-added tomato paste
1 teaspoon dried oregano
6 cups cooked spaghetti (cooked without salt
    or fat)
½ cup finely shredded zucchini
2 tablespoons grated Parmesan cheese
Fresh oregano sprigs (optional)

Coat a large nonstick skillet with cooking spray; place over medium heat until hot. Add ground beef to skillet, and cook over medium heat until browned, stirring until it crumbles. Drain and pat dry with paper towels. Wipe drippings from skillet with a paper towel.

Coat skillet with cooking spray; place over medium-high heat until hot. Add mushrooms and next 5 ingredients; sauté 5 minutes, stirring frequently. Stir in beef, tomato, water, tomato paste, and oregano. Bring to a boil; cover, reduce heat, and simmer 10 to 15 minutes or to desired consistency. Serve over cooked spaghetti; top with shredded zucchini and cheese. Garnish with fresh oregano sprigs, if desired. Yield: 6 servings.

PER SERVING: 365 CALORIES (16% FROM FAT)
FAT 6.6G (SATURATED FAT 2.4G)
PROTEIN 24.3G   CARBOHYDRATE 54.3G
CHOLESTEROL 49MG   SODIUM 412MG

Zucchini-Beef Spaghetti

CANNELLONI

1 (10-ounce) package frozen chopped spinach,
    thawed
Vegetable cooking spray
¼ cup finely chopped onion
2 cloves garlic, minced
½ pound ground round
½ pound freshly ground raw turkey
¼ cup frozen egg substitute, thawed
¼ cup plus 1 tablespoon freshly grated
    Parmesan cheese, divided
1¼ teaspoons dried Italian seasoning, divided
¼ teaspoon salt
⅛ teaspoon pepper
2 (8-ounce) cans no-salt-added tomato sauce
⅛ teaspoon salt
12 cooked manicotti shells (cooked without
    salt or fat)
White Sauce

Place spinach between paper towels, and squeeze until barely moist; set aside.

Coat a large nonstick skillet with cooking spray; place over medium heat until hot. Add onion and garlic; sauté 2 minutes. Add spinach; sauté 1 minute. Place spinach mixture in a large bowl, and set aside.

Combine ground round and turkey in skillet; cook over medium heat until browned, stirring until it crumbles. Drain and pat dry with paper towels; add to spinach mixture. Add egg substitute, 2 tablespoons Parmesan cheese, 1 teaspoon Italian seasoning, ¼ teaspoon salt, and pepper; stir well, and set aside.

Combine tomato sauce, remaining ¼ teaspoon Italian seasoning, and ⅛ teaspoon salt in a bowl, stirring well; spread 1 cup over bottom of a 13- x 9- x 2-inch baking dish coated with cooking spray.

Cannelloni

Stuff each shell with ⅓ cup spinach mixture; arrange on top of tomato sauce. Pour remaining tomato sauce over shells; spoon White Sauce evenly over tomato sauce. Sprinkle with remaining 3 tablespoons Parmesan cheese. Cover and bake at 375° for 30 minutes or until thoroughly heated. Serve immediately. Yield: 6 servings.

WHITE SAUCE

¼ cup instant nonfat dry milk powder
1 cup water
2 tablespoons margarine
2 tablespoons all-purpose flour
⅛ teaspoon salt
⅛ teaspoon ground white pepper

Combine milk powder and water; stir well, and set aside.

Melt margarine in a saucepan over medium-low heat; add flour, salt, and pepper. Cook 1 minute, stirring constantly with a wire whisk. Gradually add milk, stirring constantly. Cook, stirring constantly, an additional 10 minutes or until thickened and bubbly. (Mixture will be very thick.) Yield: 1 cup.

PER SERVING: 357 CALORIES (25% FROM FAT)
FAT 9.9G (SATURATED FAT 3.2G)
PROTEIN 28.0G   CARBOHYDRATE 38.3G
CHOLESTEROL 50MG   SODIUM 463MG

Did You Know?

Baking a recipe in a ceramic dish manufactured in another country may be dangerous. The glazes used on many ceramics often contain unhealthy levels of lead. You won't see or taste the lead, but it can leach out and contaminate food or drinks. The Food and Drug Administration checks American-made dishware to protect the public against high levels of lead. However, they have no way of checking ceramic items purchased outside the U.S. To be safe, refrain from baking or storing food in questionable ceramic ware.

CHICKEN CACCIATORE

Since French Pinot Noir can be expensive, try one from California or Oregon. Or use any dry red wine that you have on hand.

¼ teaspoon black pepper
⅛ teaspoon salt
6 chicken thighs (about 2 pounds), skinned
1 teaspoon olive oil
1 cup sliced fresh mushrooms
½ cup chopped onion
2 cloves garlic, minced
¾ cup Pinot Noir or other dry red wine
½ teaspoon dried oregano
¼ teaspoon dried crushed red pepper
2 (14½-ounce) cans plum tomatoes, undrained and chopped
6 cups cooked vermicelli (about 12 ounces uncooked), cooked without salt or fat
Fresh oregano sprigs (optional)

Sprinkle black pepper and salt over chicken thighs, and set aside.

Heat olive oil in a large nonstick skillet over medium heat. Add chicken thighs, and cook 7 minutes on each side or until lightly browned. Remove chicken thighs from skillet; cover and set aside.

Add mushrooms, onion, and garlic to skillet; sauté over medium heat 5 minutes. Add wine and next 3 ingredients; bring to a boil. Cook mixture 10 minutes or until sauce is slightly thickened, stirring occasionally.

Return chicken thighs to skillet; cover and cook 5 minutes. Uncover; turn chicken over, and cook an additional 10 minutes or until the chicken is done. Serve over vermicelli. Garnish with fresh oregano sprigs, if desired. Yield: 6 servings.

PER SERVING: 336 CALORIES (15% FROM FAT)
FAT 5.5G (SATURATED FAT 1.2G)
PROTEIN 25.7G   CARBOHYDRATE 45.4G
CHOLESTEROL 75MG   SODIUM 354MG

Beef Burgundy

BEEF BURGUNDY

2½ pounds lean, boneless round steak
Vegetable cooking spray
4 cloves garlic, minced
2 cups Burgundy or other dry red wine
1 (10¾-ounce) can condensed low-sodium,
    low-fat cream of mushroom soup,
    undiluted
1 (10½-ounce) can beef consommé, undiluted
1 (1-ounce) envelope onion recipe soup mix
6 cups sliced fresh mushrooms
1 (16-ounce) package frozen pearl onions
3 tablespoons all-purpose flour
½ cup water
2 (12-ounce) packages medium egg noodles,
    uncooked
¼ cup grated Parmesan cheese
¾ cup nonfat sour cream alternative

Trim fat from steak. Cut steak into 1-inch cubes. Coat a large, ovenproof Dutch oven with cooking spray; place over medium heat until hot. Add steak; cook 9 minutes or until steak loses its pink color. Drain well; set aside. Wipe drippings from pan with a paper towel.

Recoat pan with cooking spray; place over medium heat. Add garlic; sauté 1 minute. Add wine and next 3 ingredients; stir well, and bring to a boil. Return steak to pan; stir in mushrooms and onions. Remove from heat; set aside.

Place flour in a small bowl. Gradually add water, blending with a wire whisk; add to steak mixture. Cover and bake at 350° for 1½ hours.

Cook noodles according to package directions, omitting salt and fat. Drain well, and place in a large bowl. Add cheese and sour cream; toss gently to coat. To serve, spoon ¾ cup steak mixture over 1 cup noodles. Yield: 12 servings.

PER SERVING: 416 CALORIES (17% FROM FAT)
FAT 7.7G (SATURATED FAT 2.3G)
PROTEIN 32.8G   CARBOHYDRATE 52.5G
CHOLESTEROL 115MG   SODIUM 583MG

QUICK CASSOULET

Here's an easy version of a classic French dish that uses canned beans and cooks quickly in the microwave oven.

1 cup chopped carrot
½ cup chopped onion
½ cup canned no-salt-added beef broth,
    undiluted
2 (15.8-ounce) cans black-eyed peas, rinsed
    and drained
1 (14½-ounce) can no-salt-added whole
    tomatoes, undrained and chopped
1½ cups chopped cooked lean pork
1 cup chopped cooked chicken breast
¼ cup dry vermouth
1 teaspoon dried thyme
½ teaspoon garlic powder
½ teaspoon ground allspice
¼ teaspoon pepper
3 tablespoons toasted fine, dry breadcrumbs
2 tablespoons chopped fresh parsley

Place carrot, onion, and broth in a 3-quart casserole. Cover with heavy-duty plastic wrap and vent. Microwave at HIGH 8 minutes. Add peas and next 8 ingredients; stir well. Cover with heavy-duty plastic wrap and vent. Microwave at MEDIUM-HIGH (70% power) 13 to 15 minutes or until thoroughly heated, stirring after 7 minutes. Sprinkle with breadcrumbs and parsley. Yield: 8 servings.

PER SERVING: 224 CALORIES (20% FROM FAT)
FAT 5.1G (SATURATED FAT 0.4G)
PROTEIN 21.1G   CARBOHYDRATE 23.2G
CHOLESTEROL 42MG   SODIUM 103MG

Baking Directions: Cassoulet may be cooked conventionally, if desired. Sauté carrot and onion in a large skillet coated with cooking spray until tender. Combine sautéed vegetables, broth, and next 9 ingredients. Spoon mixture into a 3-quart casserole coated with cooking spray; cover and bake at 350° for 30 minutes or until thoroughly heated. Sprinkle with breadcrumbs and parsley.

STEAK SUKIYAKI

1 pound lean boneless top round steak
½ cup water
¼ cup low-sodium soy sauce
1 tablespoon cornstarch
2 tablespoons dry sherry
1 teaspoon peeled, minced gingerroot
½ teaspoon salt
¼ teaspoon crushed red pepper
Vegetable cooking spray
2 teaspoons vegetable oil
1 cup thinly sliced onion
¾ cup diagonally sliced celery
⅓ cup bamboo shoots
⅓ cup sliced water chestnuts
⅓ cup sliced green onions
1 cup fresh bean sprouts
1 small sweet red pepper, cut into strips
½ cup sliced fresh mushrooms
3 cups cooked long-grain rice (cooked without
    salt or fat)

Partially freeze steak; trim fat from steak. Slice steak diagonally across grain into ¼-inch strips. Combine water and next 6 ingredients in a small bowl; stir well, and set aside.

Coat a wok or large nonstick skillet with cooking spray; add oil. Heat at medium-high (375°) until hot. Add steak, and stir-fry 3 minutes. Remove steak from wok; drain and pat dry with paper towels. Wipe drippings from wok with a paper towel.

Coat wok with cooking spray; heat at medium-high until hot. Add onion and celery; stir-fry 3 minutes. Add bamboo shoots and water chestnuts; stir-fry 3 minutes. Add green onions, bean sprouts, sweet red pepper strips, and mushrooms; stir-fry 1 to 2 minutes.

Add soy sauce mixture and steak to wok. Cook, stirring constantly, until mixture is thickened and thoroughly heated. Serve steak mixture over rice. Yield: 6 servings.

PER SERVING: 282 CALORIES (21% FROM FAT)
FAT 6.6G (SATURATED FAT 2.0G)
PROTEIN 20.4G   CARBOHYDRATE 33.2G
CHOLESTEROL 48MG   SODIUM 510MG

SWEET-AND-SOUR PORK STRIPS

1 pound lean boneless pork loin
Vegetable cooking spray
1 (8-ounce) can no-salt-added tomato sauce
¼ cup rice wine vinegar
2 tablespoons brown sugar
2 teaspoons low-sodium soy sauce
¼ teaspoon minced garlic
⅛ teaspoon ground red pepper
1 (20-ounce) can pineapple chunks in juice,
    undrained
1 medium-size green pepper, seeded and cut
    into 1-inch pieces
¼ cup chopped green onions
2 tablespoons cornstarch
2 cups cooked long-grain rice (cooked without
    salt or fat)
Pepper triangles (optional)

Partially freeze pork; trim fat from pork. Slice pork diagonally across grain into thin slices; slice into 1-inch-wide strips. Coat a nonstick skillet with cooking spray; place over medium-high heat until hot. Add pork; cook 8 minutes or until browned, stirring frequently. Remove from skillet. Drain pork, and pat dry. Wipe drippings from skillet with a paper towel.

Combine pork, tomato sauce, and next 5 ingredients in skillet; bring to a boil. Cover, reduce heat, and simmer 15 minutes or until pork is tender. Drain pineapple, reserving juice. Add enough water to juice to make 1 cup liquid. Set aside.

Add pineapple, green pepper pieces, and green onions to skillet; cover and simmer 5 to 7 minutes or until vegetables are crisp-tender. Combine cornstarch and reserved pineapple juice mixture; stir into pork mixture. Cook, stirring constantly, until thickened. Spoon pork mixture over rice. Garnish with pepper triangles, if desired. Yield: 4 servings.

PER SERVING: 445 CALORIES (24% FROM FAT)
FAT 11.8G (SATURATED FAT 3.9G)
PROTEIN 25.3G   CARBOHYDRATE 57.9G
CHOLESTEROL 73MG   SODIUM 141MG

Sweet-and-Sour Pork Strips

EASY COASTAL PAELLA

12 fresh mussels
Olive oil-flavored vegetable cooking spray
2 teaspoons olive oil
1 cup chopped onion
1 cup chopped leeks
⅔ cup chopped celery
1 tablespoon minced garlic
1 teaspoon threads of saffron
2 cups peeled, seeded, and chopped tomato
½ cup Chablis or other dry white wine
½ cup canned low-sodium chicken broth,
    undiluted
2 (4-ounce) red snapper fillets, skinned
1 (4-ounce) monkfish fillet, cut into 8 pieces
2 cups cooked long-grain rice (cooked without
    salt or fat)
1 tablespoon plus 1 teaspoon chopped fresh
    parsley

Remove beards on mussels, and scrub shells with a brush. Discard opened, cracked, or heavy mussels (they're filled with sand).

Coat a large nonstick skillet with cooking spray; add olive oil. Place over medium-high heat until hot. Add onion and next 4 ingredients; sauté 3 minutes or until vegetables are tender. Add tomato, wine, and chicken broth; cook, uncovered, 10 minutes, stirring occasionally. Add fish and mussels to tomato mixture; cover and cook 5 minutes or until mussels are open and fish flakes easily when tested with a fork.

Place ½ cup rice in each individual serving bowl; spoon 1 cup fish mixture over each serving. Sprinkle with parsley. Yield: 4 servings.

PER SERVING: 305 CALORIES (14% FROM FAT)
FAT 4.8G (SATURATED FAT 0.8G)
PROTEIN 22.9G   CARBOHYDRATE 41.5G
CHOLESTEROL 34MG   SODIUM 141MG

Easy Coastal Paella

BLACK BEAN PICADILLO

½ cup dried black beans
2 cups water
1 pound ground round
Vegetable cooking spray
2 teaspoons vegetable oil
½ cup chopped onion
2 cloves garlic, minced
1 (14½-ounce) can no-salt-added whole
   tomatoes, undrained and chopped
1 (4-ounce) can chopped green chiles, drained
⅓ cup raisins
½ teaspoon salt
½ teaspoon pepper
½ teaspoon ground cinnamon
¼ teaspoon ground cloves
¼ teaspoon ground allspice
¼ teaspoon ground nutmeg
¼ teaspoon grated orange rind
⅛ teaspoon hot sauce
2 cups peeled, finely chopped cooking apple
3 cups cooked long-grain rice (cooked without
   salt or fat)

Sort and wash beans; place in a medium saucepan. Cover with water 2 inches above beans, and bring to a boil; cook 2 minutes. Remove from heat; cover and let stand 1 hour.

Drain beans. Add 2 cups water. Bring to a boil; cover, reduce heat, and simmer 3½ hours or until beans are tender. Drain and set aside.

Cook meat in a skillet over medium heat until browned, stirring until it crumbles. Drain in a colander; pat dry with paper towels, and set aside. Wipe drippings from skillet with a paper towel.

Coat skillet with cooking spray; add oil, and place over medium heat until hot. Add onion and garlic; sauté 2 minutes or until tender. Return meat to skillet. Add tomato and next 10 ingredients. Bring to a boil; reduce heat, and simmer, uncovered, 15 minutes. Add beans and apple; cook 10 minutes or until heated, stirring occasionally. Serve over rice. Yield: 6 (1½-cup) servings.

PER SERVING: 344 CALORIES (18% FROM FAT)
FAT 6.7G (SATURATED FAT 2.0G)
PROTEIN 22.2G   CARBOHYDRATE 49.4G
CHOLESTEROL 46MG   SODIUM 245MG

CUBAN BLACK BEANS AND RICE

1 pound dried black beans
Vegetable cooking spray
½ cup chopped onion
½ cup chopped green pepper
2 cloves garlic, minced
5 cups water
1 (6-ounce) can no-salt-added tomato paste
1 tablespoon vinegar
½ teaspoon sugar
½ teaspoon salt
½ teaspoon ground cumin
½ teaspoon hot sauce
4½ cups cooked long-grain rice (cooked
   without salt or fat)
½ cup plus 1 tablespoon (2¼ ounces) finely
   shredded 40% less-fat Cheddar cheese
½ cup plus 1 tablespoon peeled, seeded, and
   chopped tomato
½ cup plus 1 tablespoon chopped green onions

Sort and wash beans; place in a large Dutch oven. Cover with water to a depth of 2 inches above beans; let soak 8 hours. Drain well.

Coat a small nonstick skillet with cooking spray; place over medium-high heat until hot. Add onion, green pepper, and garlic; sauté until tender.

Combine beans, sautéed onion mixture, 5 cups water, and next 6 ingredients in pan; bring to a boil. Cover, reduce heat, and simmer 1½ hours or until beans are tender, stirring occasionally.

Place ½ cup rice in each individual serving bowl. Spoon 1 cup beans over rice, and top each serving with 1 tablespoon each of cheese, tomato, and green onions. Yield: 9 servings.

PER SERVING: 341 CALORIES (6% FROM FAT)
FAT 2.2G (SATURATED FAT 0.8G)
PROTEIN 15.8G   CARBOHYDRATE 66.5G
CHOLESTEROL 4MG   SODIUM 184MG

Curried Beef and Rice

CURRIED BEEF AND RICE

1 pound lean, boneless sirloin steak
1 tablespoon curry powder
½ teaspoon salt
⅛ teaspoon ground red pepper
1 teaspoon vegetable oil
1 cup coarsely chopped onion
2 cloves garlic, minced
1 cup long-grain rice, uncooked
1 cup no-salt-added beef broth, undiluted
½ cup raisins
1 (14½-ounce) can no-salt-added stewed
　　tomatoes, undrained
2 tablespoons sliced almonds, toasted

Trim fat from sirloin steak. Cut steak into ¾-inch cubes.

Combine curry powder, salt, and red pepper; stir well. Reserve 1 teaspoon curry mixture; set aside.

Sprinkle remaining curry mixture evenly over steak cubes.

Heat oil in a large nonstick skillet over medium-high heat. Add steak; cook 4 minutes or until steak loses its pink color. Remove steak from skillet; set aside. Add onion and garlic to skillet; cook 2 minutes. Add reserved 1 teaspoon curry mixture, rice, and next 3 ingredients; bring to a boil. Cover, reduce heat, and simmer 25 minutes or until liquid is absorbed.

Return steak to skillet; stir well. Remove from heat; let stand, covered, 5 minutes. Spoon onto individual serving plates; top with sliced almonds. Yield: 6 (1-cup) servings.

PER SERVING: 309 CALORIES (18% FROM FAT)
FAT 6.1G (SATURATED FAT 1.7G)
PROTEIN 20.4G　CARBOHYDRATE 42.9G
CHOLESTEROL 46MG　SODIUM 257MG

INDEX

METRIC EQUIVALENTS

Metric Equivalents for Different Types of Ingredients

A standard cup measure of a dry or solid ingredient will vary in weight depending on the type of ingredient. A standard cup of liquid is the same volume for any type of liquid. Use the following chart when converting standard cup measures to grams (weight) or milliliters (volume).

Standard Cup	Fine Powder (ex. flour)	Grain (ex. rice)	Granular (ex. sugar)	Liquid Solids (ex. butter)	Liquid (ex. milk)
1	140 g	150 g	190 g	200 g	240 ml
¾	105 g	113 g	143 g	150 g	180 ml
⅔	93 g	100 g	125 g	133 g	160 ml
½	70 g	75 g	95 g	100 g	120 ml
⅓	47 g	50 g	63 g	67 g	80 ml
¼	35 g	38 g	48 g	50 g	60 ml
⅛	18 g	19 g	24 g	25 g	30 ml

Useful Equivalents for Liquid Ingredients by Volume

¼ tsp						=	1 ml
½ tsp						=	2 ml
1 tsp						=	5 ml
3 tsp	=	1 tbls			=	½ fl oz	=	15 ml
		2 tbls	=	⅛ cup	=	1 fl oz	=	30 ml
		4 tbls	=	¼ cup	=	2 fl oz	=	60 ml
		5⅓ tbls	=	⅓ cup	=	3 fl oz	=	80 ml
		8 tbls	=	½ cup	=	4 fl oz	=	120 ml
		10⅔ tbls	=	⅔ cup	=	5 fl oz	=	160 ml
		12 tbls	=	¾ cup	=	6 fl oz	=	180 ml
		16 tbls	=	1 cup	=	8 fl oz	=	240 ml
		1 pt	=	2 cups	=	16 fl oz	=	480 ml
		1 qt	=	4 cups	=	32 fl oz	=	960 ml
						33 fl oz	=	1000 ml = 1 l

Useful Equivalents for Dry Ingredients by Weight

(To convert ounces to grams, multiply the number of ounces by 30.)

1 oz	=	¹⁄₁₆ lb	=	30 g
4 oz	=	¼ lb	=	120 g
8 oz	=	½ lb	=	240 g
12 oz	=	¾ lb	=	360 g
16 oz	=	1 lb	=	480 g

Useful Equivalents for Cooking/Oven Temperatures

	Fahrenheit	Celcius	Gas Mark
Freeze Water	32° F	0° C	
Room Temperature	68° F	20° C	
Boil Water	212° F	100° C	
Bake	325° F	160° C	3
	350° F	180° C	4
	375° F	190° C	5
	400° F	200° C	6
	425° F	220° C	7
	450° F	230° C	8
Broil			Grill

Useful Equivalents for Length

(To convert inches to centimeters, multiply the number of inches by 2.5.)

1 in					=	2.5 cm
6 in	=	½ ft			=	15 cm
12 in	=	1 ft			=	30 cm
36 in	=	3 ft	=	1 yd	=	90 cm
40 in					=	100 cm = 1 m